# SUPER
# SHARK
## ENCYCLOPEDIA

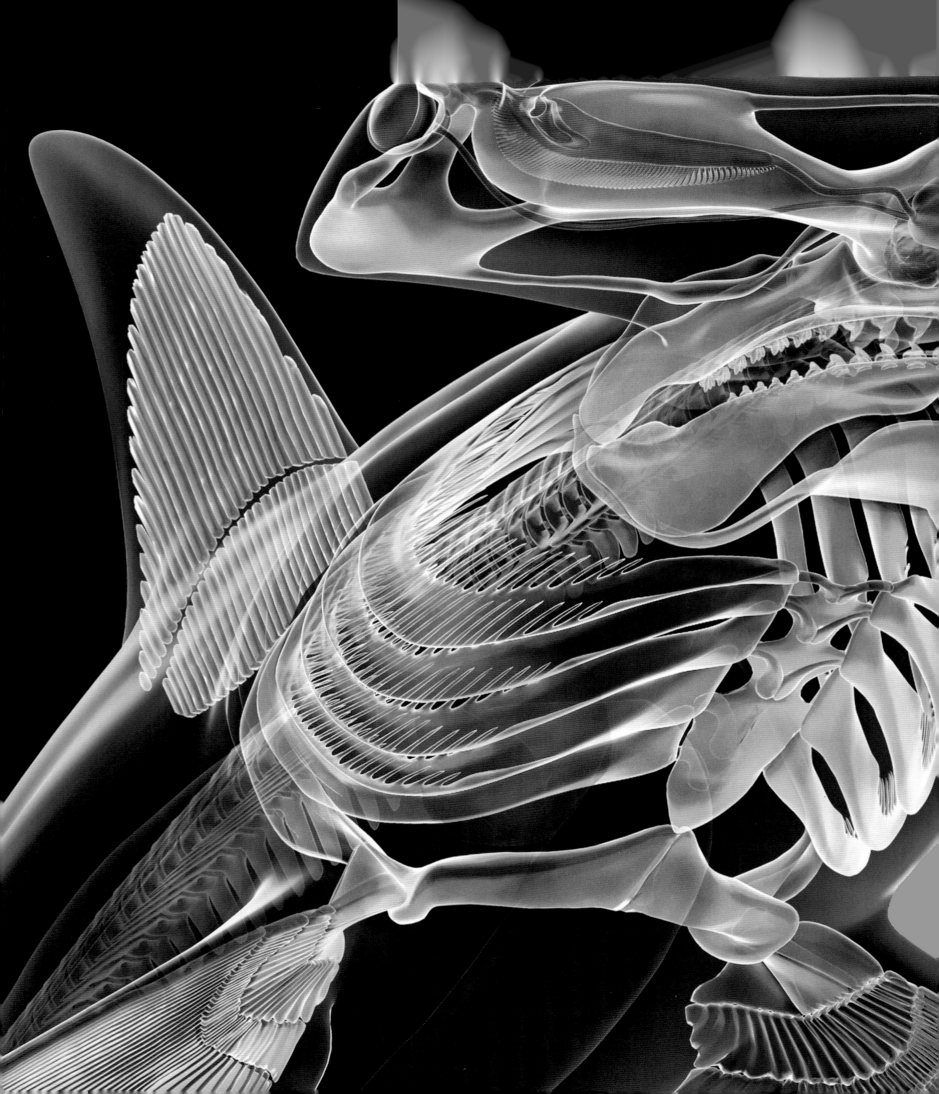

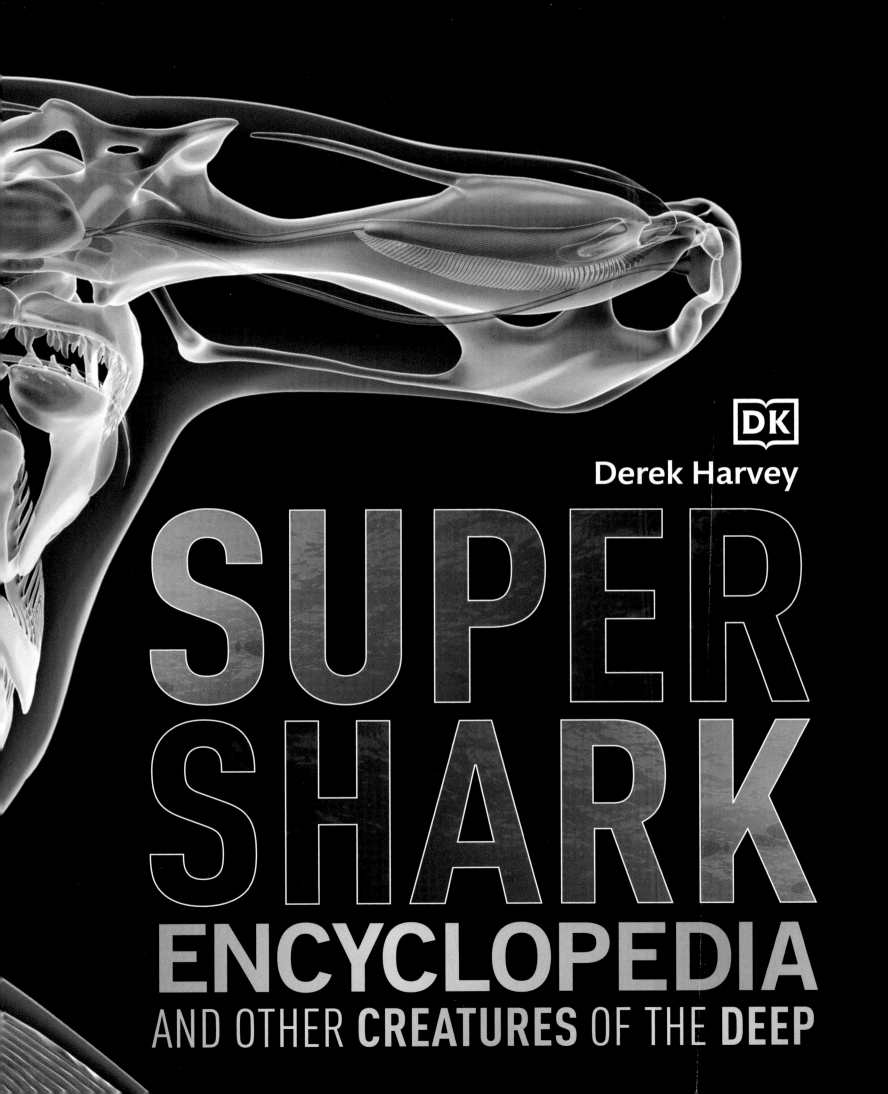

**DK**

Derek Harvey

# SUPER SHARK

# ENCYCLOPEDIA

## AND OTHER **CREATURES** OF THE **DEEP**

# CONTENTS

**DK LONDON**

**Senior Art Editor**
Anna Hall

**Senior Editors**
Janet Mohun, Wendy Horobin

**Project Art Editor**
Duncan Turner

**Editor**
Kaiya Shang

**Creative Technical Support**
Tom Morse

**US Editor**
Jill Hamilton

**Pre-production Producer**
Adam Stoneham

**Editorial Consultant**
Kim Dennis-Bryan

**Senior Producer**
Mary Slater

**DK**  Penguin Random House

**Managing Art Editors**
Michelle Baxter, Michael Duffy

**Managing Editor**
Angeles Gavira

**Deputy Art Director**
Karen Self

**Associate Publishing Director**
Liz Wheeler

**Art Director**
Philip Ormerod

**Publishing Director**
Jonathan Metcalf

**DK INDIA**

**Project Art Editors**
Isha Nagar, Vaibhav Rastogi

**Project Editor**
Bharti Bedi

**Designers**
Ranjita Bhattacharji, Divya PR, Anjali Sanchar

**Managing Editor**
Kingshuk Ghoshal

**Managing Art Editor**
Govind Mittal

**Pre-production Manager**
Balwant Singh

**DTP Designers**
Dheeraj Singh, Syed MD Farhan

**Production Manager**
Pankaj Sharma

## LIFE STORIES   90

**Living in the sea is challenging,** so an animal needs to find the best way to survive. For krill or sardines, there's safety in numbers against hungry fish. More extreme strategies involve parrotfish covering themselves in slime and sea cucumbers squirting their insides at attackers.

## SUPERNATURAL SENSES   162

**Some sea creatures** have secret superpowers. Hammerheads and sawsharks pick up electrical signals, while mantis shrimp can detect light that other animals cannot see. Sandtigers gang up on other fish and sevengill sharks sneak up on their victims, but torpedo rays have a really nasty shock in store.

## EXPLORING THE DEEP   188

**The deep sea** is the only place on Earth that remains largely unexplored. Travel from the warm shallows of a coral reef to the cold, dark bottom of the ocean in a submersible to see what lies below the waves.

**ILLUSTRATORS**

Medi-Mation
Medical & Scientific Visualization

**Creative Director**   **Senior 3D Artist**
Rajeev Doshi   Arran Lewis

**CONSULTANTS**

scubazoo

First American Edition, 2015
Published in the United States
by DK Publishing
1450 Broadway, Suite 801, New York, NY 10018
Copyright © 2015 Dorling Kindersley Limited
DK, a Division of Penguin Random House LLC
21 22 23 11 12 13 14 15 16 17
029—277085—Jun/2015

Published in Great Britain by
Dorling Kindersley Limited.

A catalog record for this book is available from the Library of Congress.
ISBN 978-1-4654-3584-2

DK books are available at special discounts when purchased in bulk for sales promotions, premiums, fund-raising, or educational use. For details, contact:
DK Publishing Special Markets,
1450 Broadway, Suite 801, New York,
New York 10018
SpecialSales@dk.com

Printed and bound in China

For the curious
www.dk.com

# TEEMING WITH LIFE

**From seashore rock pools to the wide open waters** and the deep sea beneath, the world's oceans contain an astonishing variety of life and habitats. Some animals stay so close to land that they have to move with the tides. Others spend all their lives in mid-water or prefer to crawl along the sea floor.

Coral reefs are home to a wide variety of species

Sharks living near the surface are active hunters with good vision

Sharks in deeper waters save their energy for making sudden grabs at unwary prey

Some deep-sea fish use light to attract prey and mates

Bottom-dwelling fish crawl rather than swim

## CORAL REEFS

Coral reefs grow along shallow coastlines, where bright sunshine and tropical warmth provide exactly the right conditions for thousands of different types of ocean animals, including reef sharks, to live and grow.

## OPEN OCEAN

The wide expanses of the open sea are home to vast amounts of tiny plankton that live in its upper waters. Plankton are the start of a food chain that ends with much larger animals, such as the giant ocean sunfish and meat-eating sharks.

## POLAR SEAS

The seas around the poles are so cold that they often freeze over in winter. Under the ice, the ocean is rich in nutrients and oxygen. This supports a wealth of animals, including seals and penguins that rest or breed on nearby land. Fish grow slowly because of the cold, and many have bodies packed with antifreeze chemicals.

Seabirds rely on the ocean as a source of food

Sailfish and dolphins may leap out of the water when chasing fish

Filter feeders, such as manta rays, feed on tiny animals in the plankton

Some fish bury themselves in mud and sand to ambush prey

Hydrothermal vents are places where hot water erupts from the ocean floor, and are home to many unique species

## ON THE SEASHORE

Where the ocean meets the land, marine life has to cope with the movement of the tides. Some animals stay put at low tide and wait for the water to return. Others have to swim out with the tide. The crash of waves on the seashore can be extremely powerful, and animals such as marine iguanas and crabs need to be able to grip the rocks or hide in crevices to avoid being washed away.

Large schools of fish provide food for many coastal predators

## COASTAL WATERS

Deep-water nutrients rise to the surface along coastlines, providing vital nourishment to ocean life. There is so much food that schooling fish collect there, making them a tempting target for sharks. Many people around the world use these schooling fish as a source of food.

## DEEP SEA

The deepest parts of the ocean are dark, cold, and under high pressure. The animals that live there, such as this deep-sea octopus, scavenge on dead material falling from above, or wait in the dark to ambush another animal.

### Water world

From the bright, choppy surface to the eerily dark bottom of the ocean, animals have adapted to live with the local conditions. Every layer has its own community of ocean animals, even in places where food is scarce.

# AMAZING ANATOMY

Animals that live in the ocean are supremely adapted to their wet, watery world. Fins and flippers, spikes and stingers, terrifying teeth, and your own set of headlights are just some of the things you need to survive in the sea. After all, you never know what's lurking in the depths.

# PLANKTON PLUNDERER
## BASKING SHARK

**When you're the size of a fishing boat**, it takes a lot of food to fill you. Having a big mouth helps. The basking shark cruises along with its mouth wide open like a funnel. As water flows over its gills, their bristles rake out anything from little shrimp to fish eggs—all of which is swallowed.

## AT A GLANCE

- **SIZE** Males 13–16 ft (4–5 m) long; females 26–33 ft (8–10 m) long

- **HABITAT** Coastal and open ocean waters, especially where there are large concentrations of plankton

- **LOCATION** Worldwide, except for the tropics

- **DIET** Plankton, small fish, and fish eggs

## STATS AND FACTS

**WEIGHT**

2,200 lb/1,000 kg (max. liver weight)

| lb | 3,000 | 6,000 | 9,000 |
|----|-------|-------|-------|
| kg | 1,500 | 3,000 | 4,500 |

8,800 lb/4,000 kg (max. body weight)

**50 YEARS** LIFESPAN

**WATER FILTERED**

| tons | 1,000 | 2,000 | 3,000 |
|------|-------|-------|-------|
| tonnes | 1,000 | 2,000 | 3,000 |

approx. 2,200 tons/ 2,000 tonnes (per hour)

The basking shark's giant oily liver makes it very buoyant in water, which helps it stay near the surface and travel long distances with minimal effort.

**MIGRATION DISTANCE**

| miles | 2,000 | 4,000 | 6,000 |
|-------|-------|-------|-------|
| km | 4,000 | 8,000 | 12,000 |

More than 5,600 miles (9,000 km)

MAXIMUM SCHOOL SIZE
**100**

## MASSIVE MOUTH
This shark basks near the brightly lit surface, where the water is rich in nutrients. Unlike other plankton feeders, it cannot gulp water but needs the constant stream created as it swims along.

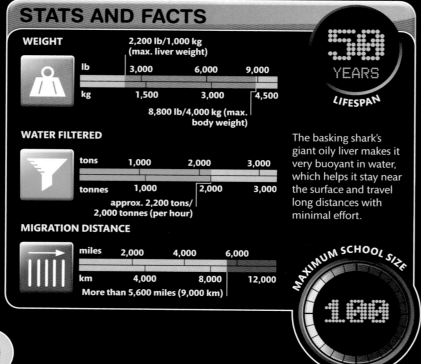

"Its **open mouth** is so **big** a child could **stand up** in it"

**NOT STRAIGHT-FACED**
One of the clues that a lefteye flounder is really lying on the right side of its body is the odd position of its mouth—which ends up strangely off-center. Its left side is colored to match the seabed.

# SHIFTY EYES
## LEFTEYE FLOUNDERS

**It takes time to turn into a flatfish** like a flounder. There is nothing especially unusual about baby flounders: they swim in the open sea with one eye on each side of their head just like most other fish. But as weeks of growth go by, one eye shifts upward and over the head—until it joins the other one on the opposite side. In lefteye flounders both eyes end up on the left side of the fish. The flounder then settles on the seabed on its eyeless right side and lives the rest of its life with both eyes facing up into the water.

### AT A GLANCE

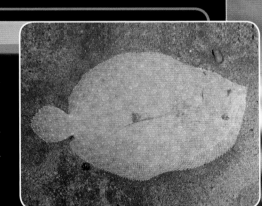

- **SIZE** 2½–35 in (6–90 cm) long
- **HABITAT** Coastal marine waters, on the ocean bed; adults migrate into the open ocean to lay eggs
- **LOCATION** Oceans worldwide
- **DIET** Bottom-living invertebrates and fish

### STATS AND FACTS

**TIME TAKEN TO TRANSFORM**

2–21 days

| days | 5 | 10 | 15 | 20 | 25 |

Some species of adult flounders settle in deeper waters than others. All of them live on sand or mud, often buried for their protection.

**DEPTH**

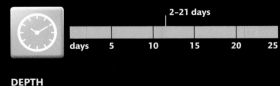

| ft | 600 | 1,200 | 1,800 |
| m | 200 | 400 | 600 |

33–660 ft/10–200 m (usual)     1,640 ft/500 m (max.)

# POP-OUT JAWS

## GIANT MORAY EEL

**The moray eel waits patiently in the darkness** of its rocky lair until a fish passes by. Then it strikes in an instant, but in a way that is not like any other reef-dwelling animal. First, its sharp-toothed mouth grabs the prey. Then, a second set of jaws shoots forward from the back of its throat to pull the fish into its food pipe.

Long spine gives the body of a moray eel snakelike flexibility

### AT A GLANCE

**SIZE** Up to 9¾ ft (3 m)

**HABITAT** Tropical reefs, especially near steep drop-offs

**LOCATION** Red Sea, East Africa, Southeast Asia, Australasia, and the western Pacific Ocean

**DIET** Mainly fish, but sometimes shrimp and crabs

### Double-jawed ambush

Moray eels can't chase prey far, so they rely on their two sets of snapping jaws to make sure a struggling fish never escapes their grasp.

Bony rods support the long dorsal fin running down the back

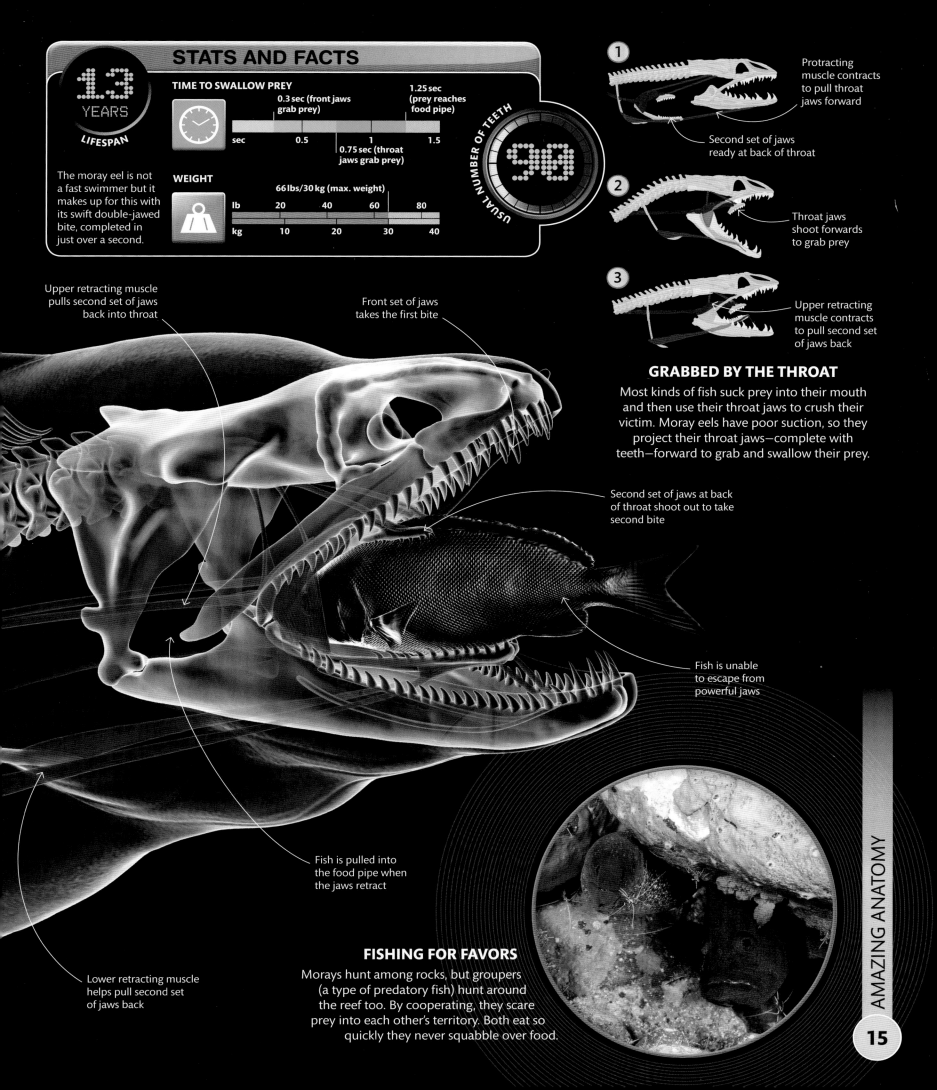

## STATS AND FACTS

### 13 YEARS LIFESPAN

The moray eel is not a fast swimmer but it makes up for this with its swift double-jawed bite, completed in just over a second.

**TIME TO SWALLOW PREY**

| sec | 0.5 | | 1 | 1.5 |
|---|---|---|---|---|

0.3 sec (front jaws grab prey)

0.75 sec (throat jaws grab prey)

1.25 sec (prey reaches food pipe)

**WEIGHT**

66 lbs/30 kg (max. weight)

| lb | 20 | 40 | 60 | | 80 |
|---|---|---|---|---|---|
| kg | 10 | 20 | | 30 | 40 |

**USUAL NUMBER OF TEETH**

98

1. Protracting muscle contracts to pull throat jaws forward

Second set of jaws ready at back of throat

2. Throat jaws shoot forwards to grab prey

3. Upper retracting muscle contracts to pull second set of jaws back

## GRABBED BY THE THROAT

Most kinds of fish suck prey into their mouth and then use their throat jaws to crush their victim. Moray eels have poor suction, so they project their throat jaws—complete with teeth—forward to grab and swallow their prey.

Upper retracting muscle pulls second set of jaws back into throat

Front set of jaws takes the first bite

Second set of jaws at back of throat shoot out to take second bite

Fish is unable to escape from powerful jaws

Fish is pulled into the food pipe when the jaws retract

Lower retracting muscle helps pull second set of jaws back

## FISHING FOR FAVORS

Morays hunt among rocks, but groupers (a type of predatory fish) hunt around the reef too. By cooperating, they scare prey into each other's territory. Both eat so quickly they never squabble over food.

# WALKING CRAB-CRUNCHER
## CALIFORNIA HORN SHARK

**With a head like a bull's and a pig-shaped snout,** the horn shark doesn't look like a ferocious killer. Its teeth are for crunching, rather than slicing, but its jaws are as strong as they come—perfect for tackling hard-shelled crabs and snails. It leaves most other animals well alone. But watch out if you ever catch a bullhead in your net: this small and gentle shark has two stinging spines on its back!

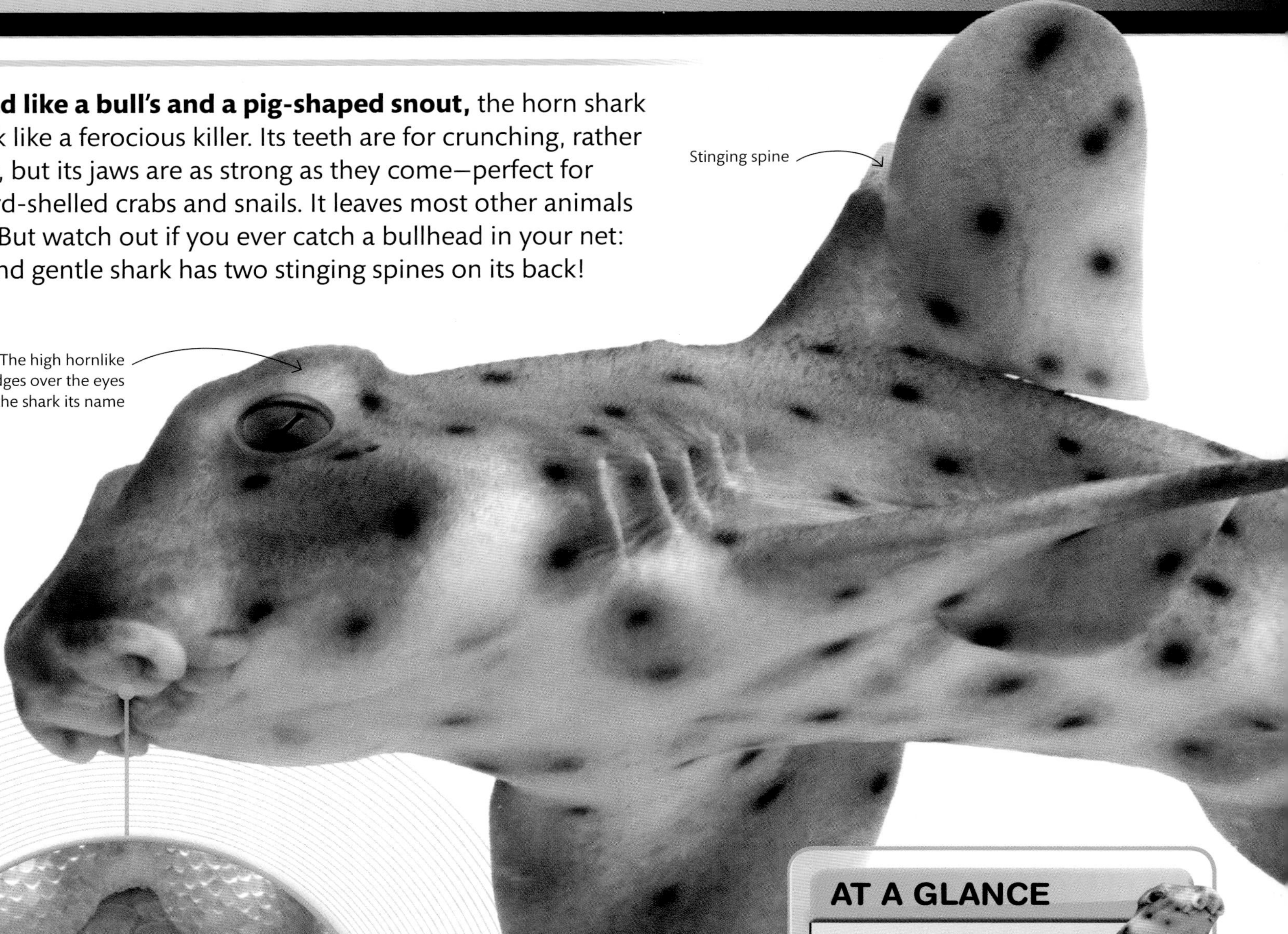

Stinging spine

The high hornlike ridges over the eyes give the shark its name

Paddlelike pectoral fins

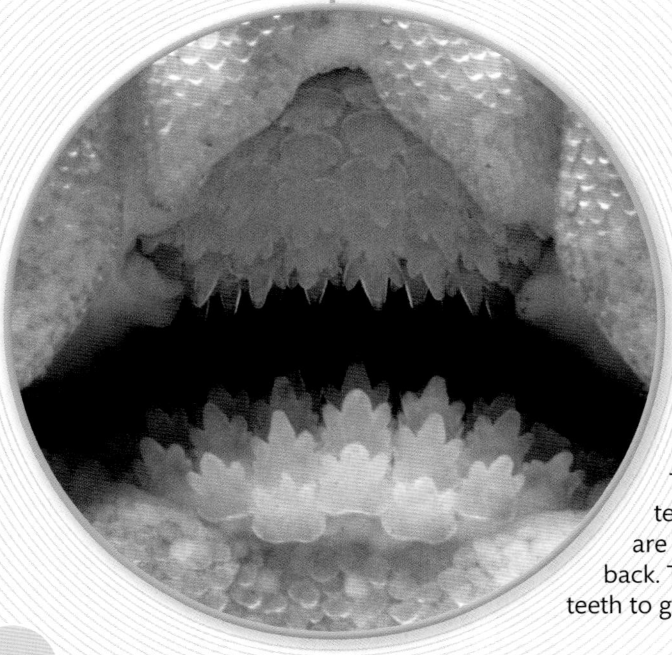

### CRUNCHING TEETH
The small mouth has small jagged teeth at the front for biting. There are stronger, broader teeth farther back. These work like our own back teeth to grind up hard food.

### AT A GLANCE

**SIZE** 23–48 in (58–122 cm)

**HABITAT** Coastal waters, especially among rocks or thick seaweed

**LOCATION** California

**DIET** Bottom-living snails, crabs, sea urchins, and small fish, hunted at night

## WALKING PREDATOR

The two paired fins at the front of the body are used for swimming, but in very shallow water they work like stumpy legs to crawl over rocks.

### STATS AND FACTS

Like many sharks of the shallows, the horn shark is built more for clambering over the bottom than for chasing prey around in open water.

**LENGTH OF FIN SPINES**

| in | | 1 | | 2 | | 3 |
|----|---|---|---|---|---|---|
| cm | 2 | | 4 | | 6 | 8 |

1¼–2¼ in (3–6 cm)

**SWIMMING DEPTH**

| ft | | 10 | 20 | 30 | 40 |
|----|---|----|----|----|----|
| m | 3 | 6 | | 9 | 12 |

6½–36 ft (2–11 m)

**SWIMMING SPEED**

| mph | | | 1 | | 2 | |
|-----|---|---|---|---|---|---|
| km/h | 1 | | 2 | 3 | | 4 |

2¼ mph (3.6 km/h)

**TIME TAKEN TO GRAB PREY**

1:10 SEC

Stinging spine

Dorsal fin

# "For its size, the horn shark has the strongest bite of any shark"

Pattern of dark brown spots helps shark with camouflage on sea floor

### EGG CASES

Most types of sharks give birth to live young, but the horn shark lays eggs in a soft leathery "purse." For extra protection, the mother picks up the case with her mouth and wedges it into a rocky crevice—where its corkscrew shape helps keep it securely in place. Over a few days it hardens to form a protective casing. This prevents predators from getting to the egg case. It will take at least six months for the young sharks to hatch.

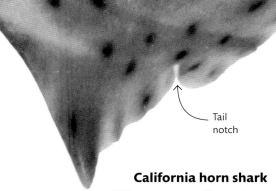

Tail notch

### California horn shark

Different species of horn sharks are found around the world and most have a distinctive pattern of dark markings on a lighter background. The California horn shark's skin is spotted.

AMAZING ANATOMY

**17**

# DEVIL OF THE DEEP
## DEEP-SEA ANGLERFISH

**The deep sea is so vast and dark** that meat eaters sometimes struggle to find prey. The anglerfish has its own way to draw them out of the gloom—it carries a glowing lantern. Other fish can't resist inspecting the light. When an especially inquisitive one comes close, the anglerfish grabs at it with its massive jaws. Its long, stabbing teeth ensure that the unsuspecting fish doesn't get away.

Waving movements of the dorsal fin help the anglerfish swim along

## AT A GLANCE

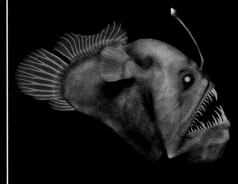

**SIZE** 3–7 in (8–18 cm) long; males ¾–1 in (2–2.8 cm) long

**HABITAT** Deep sea; larvae live nearer the surface

**LOCATION** Oceans all around the world

**DIET** Fish and other animals of the deep sea

Flexible skeleton to cope with pressure in deep water

## STATS AND FACTS

**SWIMMING DEPTH**

| ft | 5,000 | 10,000 | 15,000 |
|---|---|---|---|
| m | 1,000 2,000 | 3,000 4,000 | 5,000 |

330–4,900 ft (100–1,500 m)   14,800 ft/4,500 m (max.)

**SIZE**

Size of anglerfish 2½ in (6 cm)

Size of viperfish prey 9½ in (24 cm)

Food is so rare in the deep sea that an anglerfish needs to be able to tackle large prey. One anglerfish that was not even fully grown was found with a viperfish four times the length of its own body in its stomach.

"Its round body makes it **wobble** as it swims"

## HANGER-ON

Females also use their lantern to attract a mate. Male anglerfish do not feed, so they cannot grow as big as the females. Instead, once they have found a female, they latch onto her to fertilize her eggs. Males of some species of deep-sea anglerfish even stick to the female permanently, surviving on nourishment provided by her body.

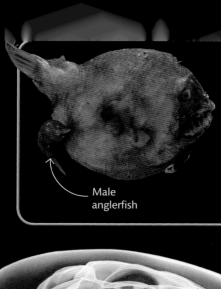

Male anglerfish

Short tube directs light outward like a flashlight

Seawater flowing in is the source of bacteria

Bacteria living in the capsule produce light

Eyes have extra-large pupils for letting in as much light as possible

Lure sits at the top of a long spine

## LURING THEM IN

A fleshy "lantern" dangles from a stalk on the anglerfish's head. It contains a thick soup of bacteria that enter the lantern from the surrounding seawater. These bacteria use chemicals produced by the fish to glow.

Long, slightly curved teeth work like fangs for stabbing prey

Massive lower jaw can open wide to swallow large prey

The black skin lacks shiny scales, so it absorbs the light given off by the lure, making it invisible to prey

Stomach expands to hold large prey

### Luminous lady

This big-mouthed anglerfish is female. Males are much smaller and do not carry lanterns. Like many other deep-sea fish, anglerfish have black skin to blend in with the background

## TUSKS TOGETHER

Like many other whales and dolphins, narwhals socialize with one another and live in groups called pods. Sometimes several hundred narwhals from different pods will gather together to form huge herds.

# UNICORN OF THE SEA
## NARWHAL

**The freezing waters of the Arctic** are home to the ocean's one-tusked wonder: the narwhal. Its tusk is really a canine tooth that grows through its upper lip. The only other tooth—a second canine—is small and useless for chewing. Instead, this white whale sucks up small animal prey from the bottom of the sea. No one knows for sure why the narwhal has a tusk, but tusks are longer in males—suggesting that they might use them for impressing the females. Sometimes narwhals have been spotted using their tusks in jousting contests.

## AT A GLANCE

- **SIZE** 13–20 ft (4–6 m) long (not including tusk)
- **HABITAT** Cold, deep ocean waters around pack ice
- **LOCATION** Arctic Ocean, mainly from Canada, Greenland, and western Russia
- **DIET** Fish, squid, and shrimp

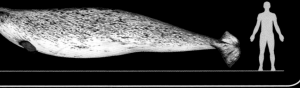

## STATS AND FACTS

**25**
MIN
MAX. DIVE DURATION

USUAL POD SIZE
UP TO

**MAXIMUM TUSK LENGTH**

| ft | 5 | 10 |
| m | 1 | 2 | 3 |

8¾ ft (2.7 m)

**MAXIMUM DIVING DEPTH**

| ft | 2,500 | 5,000 |
| m | 400 | 800 | 1,200 | 1,600 |

4,920 ft (1,500 m)

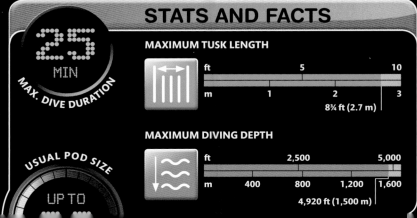

# STINGING BATTLESHIP

## PORTUGUESE MAN O' WAR

**The sting of a Portuguese man o' war** is so painful that the shock alone can kill. Although it looks like a single jellyfish, it is actually a floating colony of many animals that make up the writhing mass of tentacles hanging under the balloonlike float. Some of these produce eggs, some carry stings and grab prey. Others are tipped with tiny mouths for eating their victim.

Sail on the float catches the wind to help it move over the ocean

Gland produces gas for inflating the float

Gonozooids hang like tiny grapes and produce eggs or sperm

Gastrozooids tipped with tiny mouths (yellow) eat prey

Colony is made up of thousands of individuals called zooids

Pore opens to let gas escape, adjusting amount in the float

Gastrozooid contains fragments of partly digested food

Muscular walls help dactylozooid move to grab prey

### DEADLY COILS

The tentacles are made up of muscular dark-blue coils and long fingerlike members of the colony. They carry thousands of stingers for paralyzing prey. Then they pull the victim up to waiting hungry mouths.

# "Each harpoon fires with the pressure of a bullet"

Dactylozooids grab prey and are entwined with stinging tentacles

Tentacles have beadlike clumps of stingers

Stingers remain dangerous even if tentacle is broken off

## Working together

Members of this floating colony have different functions but they all work together as one. Many form long chains that hang down to sting and catch prey. Up nearer the float are shorter ones with mouths. As prey is dragged close, these reach out to suck and digest the flesh of the victim.

## HARPOON IN MINIATURE

You would need a microscope to see the tiny stingers in the skin of a tentacle. When touched, the stinger fires a venomous harpoon into the prey's flesh. Hundreds of stingers fire at once, causing excruciating pain.

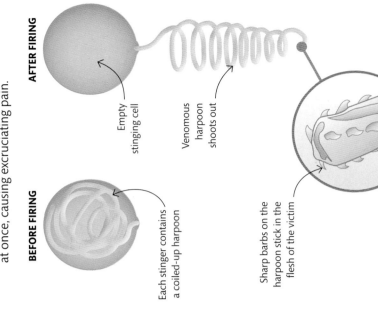

**BEFORE FIRING**

Each stinger contains a coiled-up harpoon

**AFTER FIRING**

Empty stinging cell

Venomous harpoon shoots out

Sharp barbs on the harpoon stick in the flesh of the victim

## AT A GLANCE

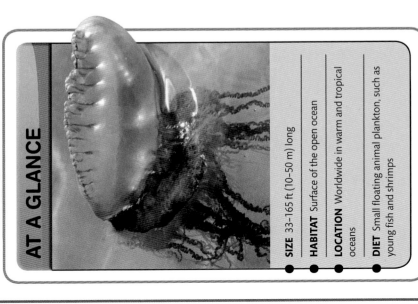

**SIZE** 33–165 ft (10–50 m) long

**HABITAT** Surface of the open ocean

**LOCATION** Worldwide in warm and tropical oceans

**DIET** Small floating animal plankton, such as young fish and shrimps

## STATS AND FACTS

**HEIGHT**

| ft | 50 | 100 | 150 | 200 |
|---|---|---|---|---|
| m | 10 | 20 | 30 | 40 | 50 | 60 |

165 ft (50 m) total length

6 in (15 cm) height of gas bladder

**SAILING SPEED**

| mph | 0.5 | 1 | 1.5 | |
|---|---|---|---|---|
| km/h | 1 | 2 | 3 |

0.25–1.6 mph (0.4–2.5 km/h)

When the wind blows on the floating "sail," the colony moves over the ocean, snagging prey as it goes. The amount of gas in the float is adjustable and affects how far the colony travels.

**DIET**

80% young fish

20% other animals

FISH CAUGHT

42 PER DAY

AMAZING ANATOMY

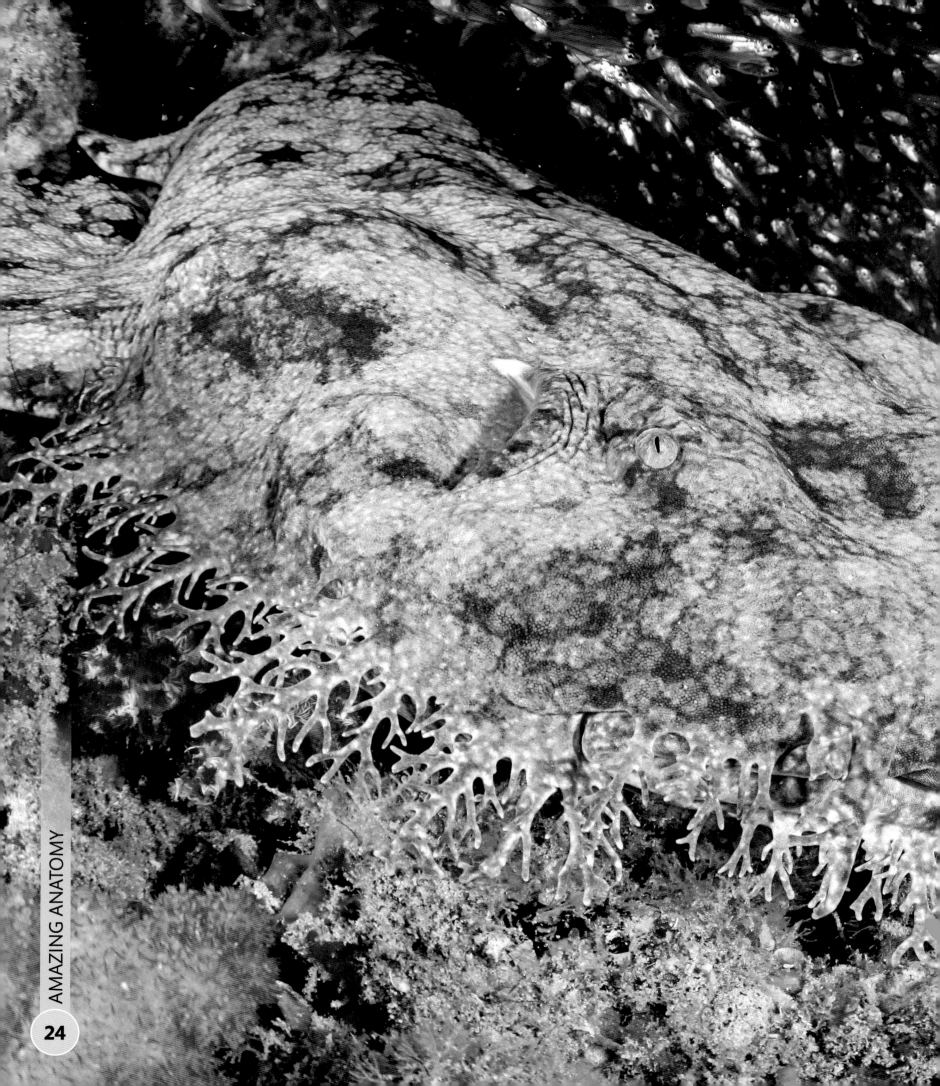

# TASSELED AMBUSHER
## WOBBEGONG

**Looking more like** a piece of shaggy seaweed than a shark, the wobbegong has the perfect way to snatch a meal. It relies on its disguise and waits for prey to come close before making a grab. Its wormlike tassels might even lure a fish in. The flattened body of this shark is not much good for building up speed in a chase, but when it comes to attacking, the wobbegong is no laggard. It can snap its jaws in the blink of an eye, and sharp needlelike teeth ensure that even the most slippery prey is trapped.

## AT A GLANCE

- **SIZE** 3¼–12 ft (1–3.6 m) long
- **HABITAT** Rocky shallow ocean waters and coral reefs
- **LOCATION** Coastlines of tropical eastern Asia and Australasia
- **DIET** Crabs, lobsters, octopuses, and bottom-living fish

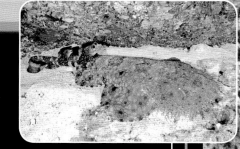

## STATS AND FACTS

The sensitive tassels of a wobbegong can detect when prey comes within its reach. Then it strikes, much faster than many other kinds of sharks.

**DEPTH**

0–165 ft /0–50 m (usual depth)

| ft | 300 | 600 | 900 |
|---|---|---|---|
| m | 100 | 200 | 300 |

720 ft/220 m (record depth)

**DIET**

12% octopus

82% bony fish

6% other sharks

TIME TO GRAB PREY

1:50 SEC

# SHELL SHEDDER
## BLUE SWIMMING CRAB

**Big crabs are heavy on land** because of their cumbersome hard shell, but they are buoyant in the ocean—and this crab even has paddles to get around in midwater. Hard shells offer good protection, but are too stiff to expand—so crabs must discard their old shell and make a new, bigger one so that they can grow.

Back legs are used for swimming

## AT A GLANCE

- **SIZE** 6½–10½ in (17–27 cm) shell diameter

- **HABITAT** Estuaries and bays with muddy or sandy bottoms, going upstream into rivers

- **LOCATION** Western North America, Gulf of Mexico south to Argentina, introduced to Europe and Japan

- **DIET** Oysters, clams, mussels, worms, small fish, seaweed, and carrion

"Only **one in a million** baby crabs survives to become an adult"

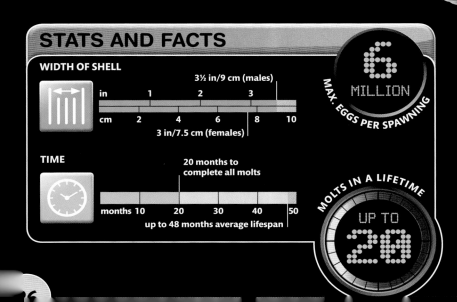

Thick muscles at the base of the claw pull on flat blades to open and close the pincers

Muscles in each leg segment work in pairs: one bends the leg, the other extends it

## STATS AND FACTS

**WIDTH OF SHELL**

3½ in/9 cm (males)

| in | 1 | 2 | 3 |
|----|---|---|---|
| cm | 2 | 4 | 6 | 8 | 10 |

3 in/7.5 cm (females)

**MAX. EGGS PER SPAWNING**
**6 MILLION**

**TIME**

20 months to complete all molts

| months 10 | 20 | 30 | 40 | 50 |

up to 48 months average lifespan

**MOLTS IN A LIFETIME**
**UP TO 20**

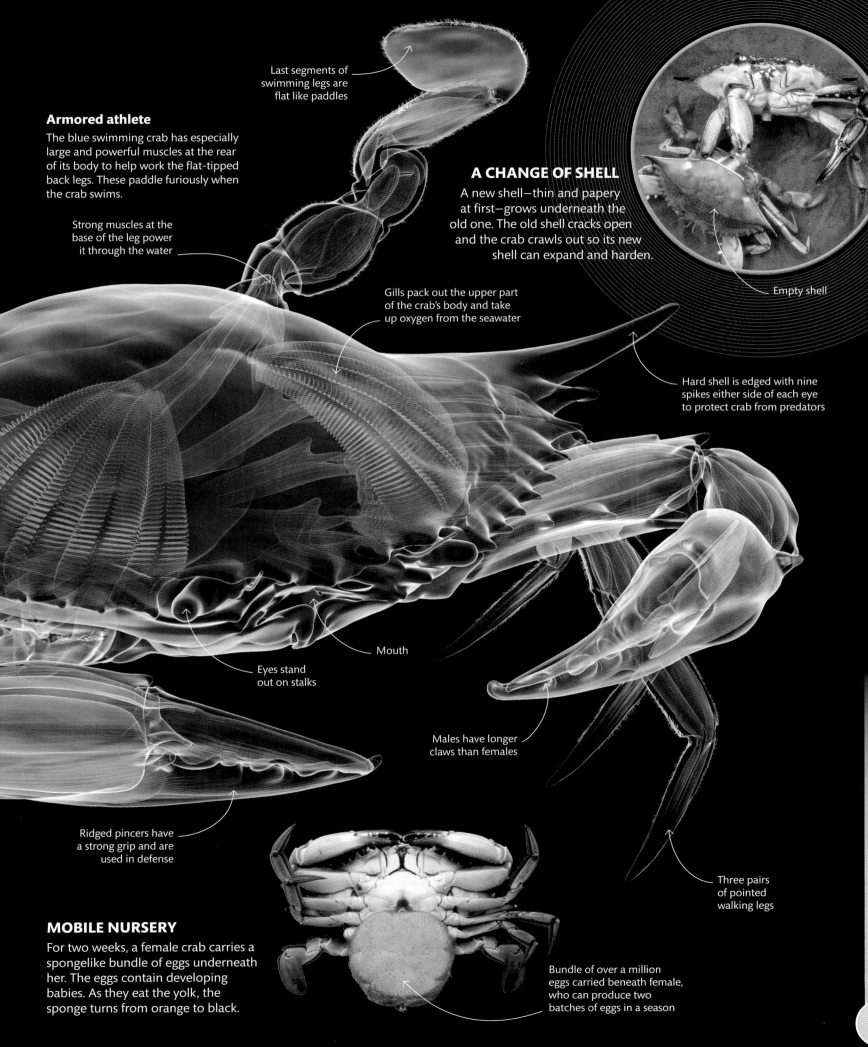

## Armored athlete

The blue swimming crab has especially large and powerful muscles at the rear of its body to help work the flat-tipped back legs. These paddle furiously when the crab swims.

Last segments of swimming legs are flat like paddles

Strong muscles at the base of the leg power it through the water

## A CHANGE OF SHELL

A new shell—thin and papery at first—grows underneath the old one. The old shell cracks open and the crab crawls out so its new shell can expand and harden.

Empty shell

Gills pack out the upper part of the crab's body and take up oxygen from the seawater

Hard shell is edged with nine spikes either side of each eye to protect crab from predators

Mouth

Eyes stand out on stalks

Males have longer claws than females

Ridged pincers have a strong grip and are used in defense

Three pairs of pointed walking legs

## MOBILE NURSERY

For two weeks, a female crab carries a spongelike bundle of eggs underneath her. The eggs contain developing babies. As they eat the yolk, the sponge turns from orange to black.

Bundle of over a million eggs carried beneath female, who can produce two batches of eggs in a season

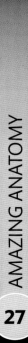

**A TINY MOUTH**

The mouth of a seahorse is like the end of a tiny trumpet. Instead of chewing, it sucks microscopic animals out of the plankton. Even these minuscule creatures are a big meal for a pygmy seahorse.

# CAMOUFLAGE IN MINIATURE
## PYGMY SEAHORSE

**Being a slowpoke is a problem on a reef** filled with speedy predators, especially when you are small enough to fit in everyone's mouth. Seahorses are among the slowest of small fish, but fortunately they are also experts at camouflage. These tiny pygmy seahorses—smaller than your little finger—are colored pink, white, and red to blend in with the coral. Their coiling tails hold fast to a coral branch, just in case a sudden current sweeps through the reef and threatens to wash them into dangerous open water.

## AT A GLANCE

**SIZE** ½–1 in (1.4–2.7 cm) long (from tip of tail to tip of snout)

**HABITAT** Tropical coral reefs, where they are camouflaged among the coral branches

**LOCATION** Tropical western Pacific coastlines, including Japan, Southeast Asia, New Guinea, Australia, and Pacific Islands

**DIET** Tiny crustaceans

## STATS AND FACTS

Most male seahorses have a pouch for brooding young, but for a pygmy seahorse a slit in the belly is good enough.

**EGG INCUBATION TIME**

11–14 days in body

| days | 5 | 10 | 15 |

**YOUNG PER BROOD**
UP TO

**SWIMMING DEPTH**

| ft | 100 | 200 | 300 |
| m | 30 | 60 | 90 | 120 |

36–295 ft (11–90 m)

# SEAWATER SWALLOWER
## SWELL SHARK

**The striped pattern on this little shark** helps it blend into the dense thickets of brown seaweed in its habitat. This usually helps hide it from the prying eyes of larger sharks, but if danger threatens it has another trick for defending itself. The shark can make its body bigger by gulping water into its stomach. It will even grab its tail with its mouth to make a U-bend with its body, making it more difficult for a predator to pull it out from rocky crevices and overhangs.

## AT A GLANCE

- **SIZE** 2½–3½ ft (0.8–1.1 m) long
- **HABITAT** Usually in shallow waters covered in a bed of kelp or other types of seaweed
- **LOCATION** Eastern Pacific Ocean off the coasts of California, Mexico, and central Chile
- **DIET** Fish, shrimp, crabs, and snails

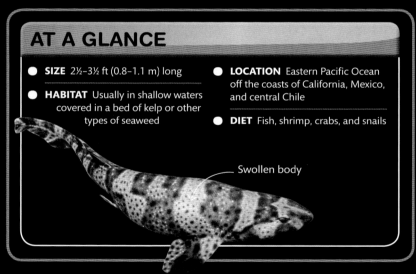

Swollen body

## STATS AND FACTS

**TIME TO SWELL**

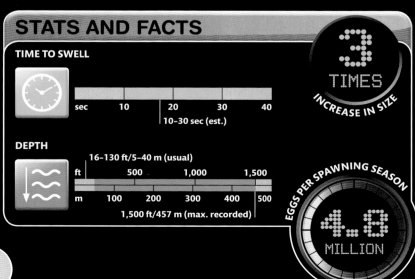

| sec | 10 | 20 | 30 | 40 |

10–30 sec (est.)

**3 TIMES**
INCREASE IN SIZE

**DEPTH**

16–130 ft/5–40 m (usual)

| ft | 500 | 1,000 | 1,500 |
| m | 100 | 200 | 300 | 400 | 500 |

1,500 ft/457 m (max. recorded)

**4.8 MILLION**
EGGS PER SPAWNING SEASON

## UNDERCOVER SHARK
Swell sharks hide among rocks and seaweed, where they can ambush small prey or hide from predators. They can even do their expanding trick when removed from the sea by swallowing air instead of water.

"The swell shark makes a **doglike bark** when releasing air"

# SPIKY PREDATOR
## LIONFISH

**A lionfish has good reason** to be confident as it swaggers around the ocean reef. Pencil-long spines stick out from its body in all directions, many spiked with venom. The lionfish is a top predator that will eat almost anything that fits into its big mouth. And if that weren't enough, its stomach can expand massively to squeeze in as much prey as possible.

Venomous spines used in self-defense

### VENOMOUS SPINES

Each spine has two grooves to carry venom. In a human, the pain from a jab can last for days. The victim gets sticky with sweat and could end up with a paralyzed limb.

### Stinging invader

The bright striped markings of a lionfish warn of danger. Lionfish are popular aquarium pets, but if released into the ocean they can devastate local wildlife.

### AT A GLANCE

- **SIZE** 8–15 in (20–38 cm)
- **HABITAT** Coral reefs, rocky outcrops, lagoons, and muddy waters
- **LOCATION** Tropical coastlines from the Indian Ocean to the central Pacific Ocean; introduced elsewhere (such as the Caribbean)
- **DIET** Fish, crabs, shrimp, snails, and other marine animals

"Whiskers" help break up outline of mouth as fish approaches prey

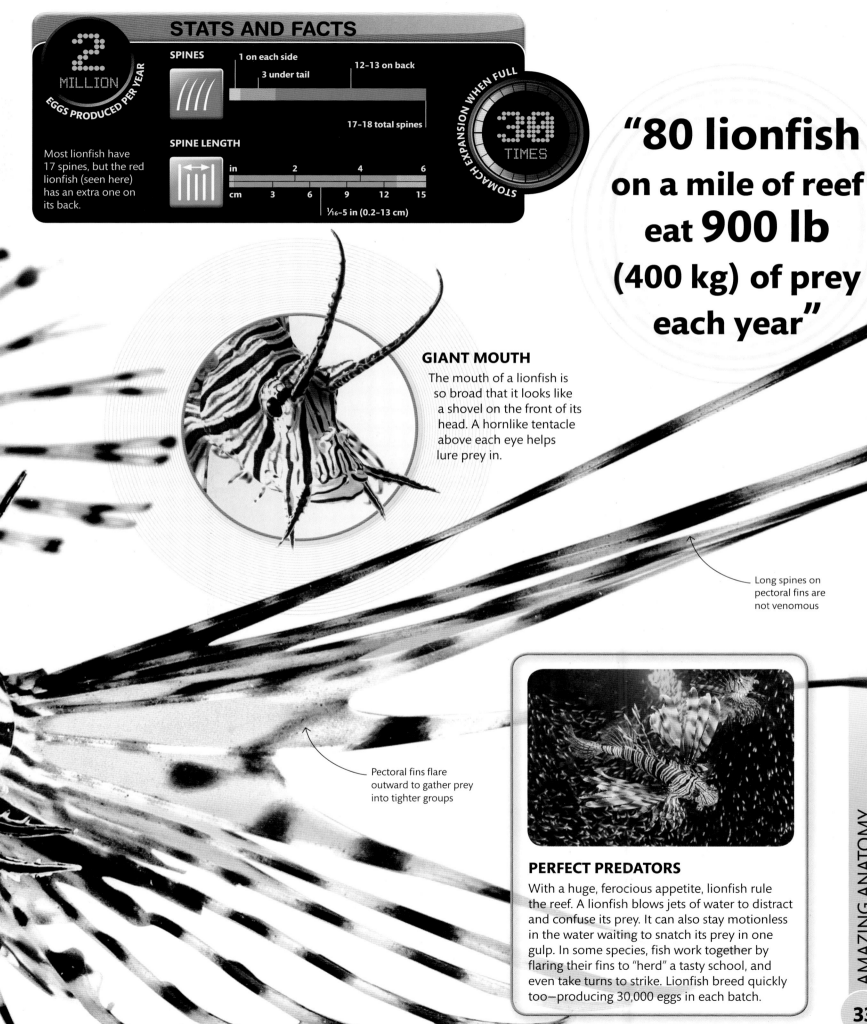

## STATS AND FACTS

**2 MILLION**
EGGS PRODUCED PER YEAR

Most lionfish have 17 spines, but the red lionfish (seen here) has an extra one on its back.

**SPINES**

1 on each side
3 under tail
12–13 on back

17–18 total spines

**SPINE LENGTH**

| in | | 2 | | 4 | | 6 |
| cm | 3 | 6 | 9 | 12 | 15 | |

1/16–5 in (0.2–13 cm)

STOMACH EXPANSION WHEN FULL

**30 TIMES**

## "80 lionfish on a mile of reef eat 900 lb (400 kg) of prey each year"

### GIANT MOUTH

The mouth of a lionfish is so broad that it looks like a shovel on the front of its head. A hornlike tentacle above each eye helps lure prey in.

Long spines on pectoral fins are not venomous

Pectoral fins flare outward to gather prey into tighter groups

### PERFECT PREDATORS

With a huge, ferocious appetite, lionfish rule the reef. A lionfish blows jets of water to distract and confuse its prey. It can also stay motionless in the water waiting to snatch its prey in one gulp. In some species, fish work together by flaring their fins to "herd" a tasty school, and even take turns to strike. Lionfish breed quickly too—producing 30,000 eggs in each batch.

AMAZING ANATOMY

33

# WHITE-BLOODED WONDER
## CROCODILE ICEFISH

**It takes a special kind of fish** to survive the deep Antarctic Ocean, where temperatures are only just above freezing. The crocodile icefish not only has built-in antifreeze, but is the only backboned animal with colorless blood. All other backboned animals need red blood cells to carry oxygen, but cold polar waters contain so much oxygen that the icefish does not need them.

Long snout is full of sharp teeth that help in grabbing prey

Massive heart helps pump extra oxygen around the body

### Bleached baby

This baby icefish looks as though its body is made from glass. In cold water, it can be hard for a fish to pump blood with lots of red cells around its body because it gets too thick, but the icefish has no red cells at all. The whiteness of its bones, muscles, and organs shows through its transparent skin.

Only the food-filled digestive system shows color

Without the redness of blood, lines of muscle appear white

## AT A GLANCE

**SIZE** 10–28 in (25–72 cm)

**HABITAT** Cold Antarctic ocean waters, near the ocean floor

**LOCATION** Coastlines of Antarctica and southern South America

**DIET** Other fish, shrimp, and crabs

## STATS AND FACTS

**HABITAT TEMPERATURE**

| °F | 28 | 32 | 36 |
|---|---|---|---|
| °C | -2 | 0 | 2 | 4 |

28.5–34.7°F (-1.9–1.5°C)

Fresh water freezes at 32°F (0°C), but in the chilly marine habitat of the crocodile icefish, the presence of salt means seawater can get much colder before it freezes.

**SWIMMING DEPTH**

| ft | 1,500 | 3,000 | 4,500 | 6,000 |
|---|---|---|---|---|
| m | 500 | 1,000 | 1,500 | 2,000 |

2,300–4,920 ft (700–1,500 m)

REACHES MATURITY IN
4–8
YEARS

*"*An icefish has **four times** as much blood as a red-blooded fish of a similar size*"*

# WINGS OF THE SEA
## ANGEL SHARK

Angel **"wings"** might make for graceful swimming, but these sharks are bad-tempered "angels." During the day, angel sharks settle on the bottom, perfectly camouflaged, and strike with lightning speed using needlelike teeth. If you accidentally tread on one, you'll see why it has the nickname of "sand devil."

### AT A GLANCE

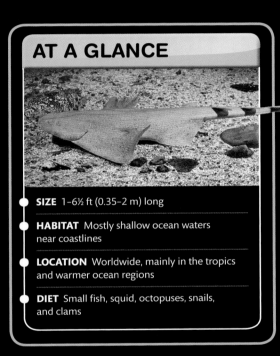

- **SIZE** 1–6½ ft (0.35–2 m) long
- **HABITAT** Mostly shallow ocean waters near coastlines
- **LOCATION** Worldwide, mainly in the tropics and warmer ocean regions
- **DIET** Small fish, squid, octopuses, snails, and clams

### STATS AND FACTS

**"WING" SPAN**

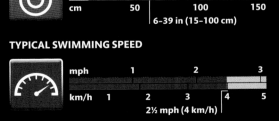

| in | | 20 | | 40 | |
|---|---|---|---|---|---|
| cm | 50 | | 100 | | 150 |

6–39 in (15–100 cm)

**TYPICAL SWIMMING SPEED**

| mph | | 1 | | 2 | | 3 |
|---|---|---|---|---|---|---|
| km/h | 1 | | 2 | 3 | | 4 | 5 |

2½ mph (4 km/h)

**STRIKE DISTANCE**

| in | | 2 | | 4 | | 6 | |
|---|---|---|---|---|---|---|---|
| cm | | | 10 | | | | 20 |

6 in (15 cm)

TIME TO STRIKE PREY

**1.0 SEC**

The angel shark cannot swim fast, so it prefers to ambush its prey. Its eyes face upward to spot anything that comes within range. Then it extends its jaws to grab its victim.

Five gill slits on the upper surface of the body

Small eyes on top of flattened head

Enlarged pectoral fins flap to help the shark swim

### Angel of death

At night, angel sharks move off the bottom and cruise the sea floor to look for food. Their "wings" are really pectoral fins that extend from either side of the body, making them look more like a ray than a shark.

Lower lobe of tail fin is bigger than upper lobe, unlike most other sharks

The first of two small dorsal fins is at the rear of the body

# HOT-BLOODED KILLER
## GREAT WHITE SHARK

**The great white shark** is the most infamous killer of them all, and a hungry great white is a speedy hunter. It has a particular taste for warm-blooded meat and often targets mammals, such as seals or dolphins. It matches their speed because it has special strips of muscle that generate its own body heat, while a clever system of blood vessels keeps the heat trapped inside.

### KILLING BLADES

The great white shark has large, sharp, triangular teeth. The narrower bottom teeth are for gripping prey, while the upper saw-edged teeth slice through flesh.

## AT A GLANCE

- **SIZE** Up to 20 ft (6 m) long

- **HABITAT** Most coastal and offshore ocean waters

- **LOCATION** Worldwide

- **DIET** Seals, dolphins, turtles, seabirds, and large fish

Sensitive snout detects electrical activity given off by prey

## STATS AND FACTS

**PREY WEIGHT**

| lb | 1,000 | 2,000 | 3,000 | |
|---|---|---|---|---|
| kg | 400 | 800 | 1,200 | 1,600 |

2¼–3,305 lb
(1–1,500 kg)

**SWIMMING DEPTH**

| ft | | 2,000 | 4,000 | |
|---|---|---|---|---|
| m | 500 | 1,000 | 1,500 |

2,950 ft/900 m (usual)  |  3,940 ft/1,200 m (record)

**RECORD DISTANCE**

12,400 miles (20,000 km)

| miles | 5,000 | 10,000 | 15,000 |
|---|---|---|---|
| km | 10,000 | 20,000 | 30,000 |

The great white shark is one of the longest-lived and most wide-ranging of any shark. Although it is more usually seen near coastlines, it often migrates long distances, sometimes crossing entire oceans to do so.

**LIFESPAN**

**70 YEARS**

Row of teeth behind main ones replace any that break off

### Super predator

Size, speed, and strong jaws all make the great white shark one of the most fearsome predators alive today. Youngsters prey on other fish but bigger adults turn to sea mammals—and sometimes attack humans. As well as living prey, great whites have also been seen scavenging whale carcasses.

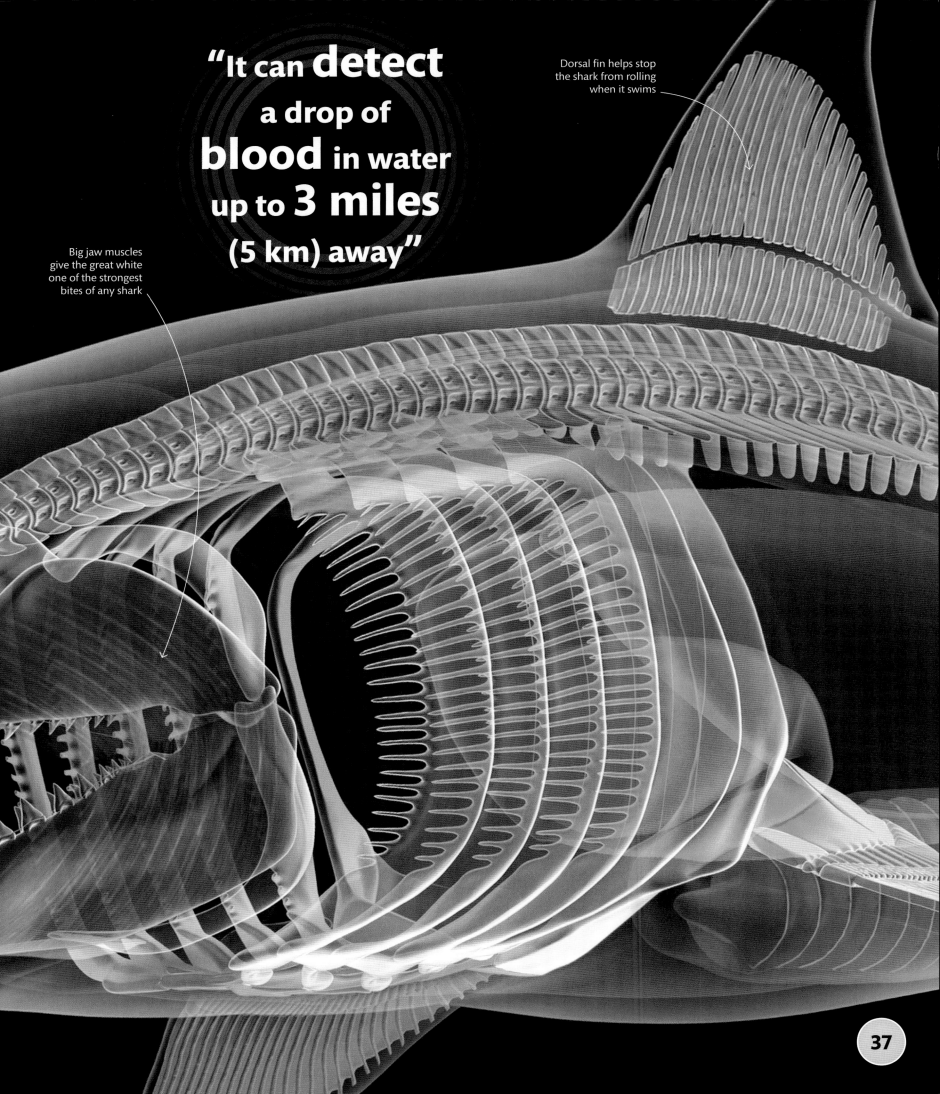

"It can **detect** a drop of **blood** in water up to **3 miles** (5 km) away"

Dorsal fin helps stop the shark from rolling when it swims

Big jaw muscles give the great white one of the strongest bites of any shark

## JUMPING JAWS

A fat seal makes a filling meal for a hungry great white shark, which is why they patrol the waters around seal colonies. The shark charges upward from below the seal so fast that it often launches into the air as it grabs its victim between its fearsome jaws. The seal is left badly wounded; a bite to the head and neck kills it quickly. The shark then drags the body below the surface to eat.

"Great white sharks can **jump** up to **10 ft (3 m)** out of the water"

# BIG-LIPPED MOLLUSK
## GIANT CLAM

**Most clams can fit on a teaspoon**, but this giant would just barely fit in your bathtub. Weighing as much as two baby elephants, with most of the weight taken up by its shell, it lives on shallow reefs. Like small clams, it is a bivalve, which means its shell is in two parts, hinged along the bottom. Strong muscles allow the shell to open and close. When gaping wide, its fleshy body can bask in the warm tropical sunshine. Light provides much of the energy needed for the clam to grow big.

### AT A GLANCE

- **SIZE** Up to 4 ft (1.2 m) long
- **HABITAT** Shallow ocean waters
- **LOCATION** Tropical oceans, mostly of the Indo-Pacific
- **DIET** Plankton and food produced by live-in algae

### STATS AND FACTS

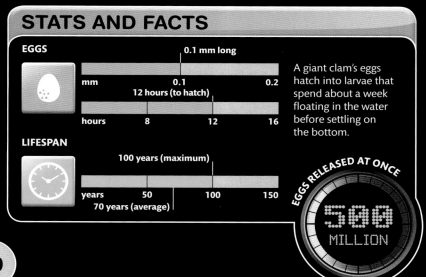

**EGGS**

0.1 mm long

| mm | 0.1 | 0.2 |

12 hours (to hatch)

| hours | 8 | 12 | 16 |

A giant clam's eggs hatch into larvae that spend about a week floating in the water before settling on the bottom.

**LIFESPAN**

100 years (maximum)

| years | 50 | 100 | 150 |

70 years (average)

EGGS RELEASED AT ONCE

**500 MILLION**

"A giant clam releases up to **6 billion eggs** during its lifetime"

**BIGGEST** SHELLED MOLLUSK

**FOOD SOURCES**
Giant clams get some food from plankton. The rest is made by microscopic algae living in their flesh that use the Sun's energy to make food—just like plants do—which they share with the clams.

# POP-UP PREDATOR
## BITING REEF WORM

**Worms often fall prey** to hungry fish, but this one breaks all the rules. It can grow to the length of a car but most of its body is hidden under the sand and only its murderous head pokes out. Should any fish swim too close, the worm attacks, slicing madly with jagged jaws that can cut a small body clean in half. It even has a knock-out poison to stop larger prey from getting away.

### AT A GLANCE

- **SIZE** 3¼–9¾ ft (1–3 m)
- **HABITAT** On tropical reefs, under boulders, in crevices, and in mud or sand
- **LOCATION** Indian Ocean and western Pacific Ocean
- **DIET** Shrimp, worms, fish, seaweed, and dead material; it emerges at night to feed

### STATS AND FACTS

**JAW SPAN**

| in | | 1 | | 2 | |
|---|---|---|---|---|---|
| cm | 2 | | 4 | | 6 |

2 in/5 cm (average)

**673**
MAXIMUM BODY SEGMENTS

**HEIGHT OUT OF BURROW**

| in | 2 | 4 | 6 | 8 | 10 |
|---|---|---|---|---|---|
| cm | 5 | 10 | 15 | 20 | 25 | 30 |

approx. 8 in/20 cm (above burrow)

The biting reef worm senses prey with the feelers on its head before taking a fast, slashing bite.

**TIME TAKEN TO STRIKE**

0.5 sec (est.)

| sec | 0.2 | 0.4 | 0.6 |
|---|---|---|---|

NUMBER OF FEELERS

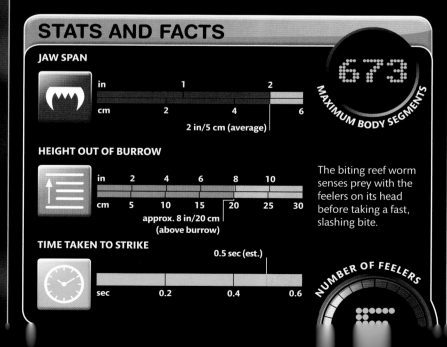

**FIERCEST WORM BITE**

### SCISSORLIKE JAWS

By firing its throat out through its mouth, the biting reef worm's jaws can reach even farther to grab its prey. The bite of the sharp, jagged jaws

"The biting reef worm has **five pairs** of fast-action **jaws**"

"This **aggressive** shark often **follows ships** in its hunt for food"

**LONG-FINNED BULLY**

The oceanic whitetip is a solitary shark, but often gathers at feeding frenzies, where it bullies the other sharks to get a better share of the food. It will also follow pods of dolphins and pilot whales to scavenge their catch.

# FABULOUS FINS
## OCEANIC WHITETIP SHARK

**The oceanic whitetip shark** likes to cruise just beneath the surface of warm tropical oceans, with its long, paddlelike fins spread outward. Despite its sedate lifestyle, it hunts some of the fastest oceanic fish, including tuna and mackerel. It swims along with its mouth wide open until prey comes close enough for it to make a grab with its jaws.

## AT A GLANCE

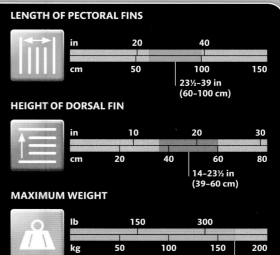

- **SIZE** 9¾–13 ft (3–4 m) long
- **HABITAT** Warm open ocean, usually near the surface
- **LOCATION** Tropical and subtropical oceans around the world
- **DIET** Mainly fish and squid, but sometimes seabirds, marine mammals, and human rubbish

## STATS AND FACTS

In proportion to its body, this shark's dorsal and pectoral fins are bigger than those of many other species of sharks. It gets its name because the rounded edges of its fins are tipped with white.

**LENGTH OF PECTORAL FINS**

| in | | 20 | | 40 | |
|----|----|----|----|----|----|
| cm | | 50 | | 100 | 150 |

23½–39 in
(60–100 cm)

**HEIGHT OF DORSAL FIN**

| in | | 10 | | 20 | | 30 |
|----|----|----|----|----|----|----|
| cm | | 20 | 40 | | 60 | 80 |

14–23½ in
(39–60 cm)

**MAXIMUM WEIGHT**

| lb | | 150 | | 300 | |
|----|----|----|----|----|----|
| kg | | 50 | 100 | 150 | 200 |

368 lb (167 kg)

MAXIMUM LIFESPAN
22 YEARS

# SHARPSHOOTER
## CONE SNAIL

**A slow snail has to have a secret weapon** to catch a fish, and the cone snail is the most dangerous snail of all. Like its vegetarian cousins, it has a single creeping foot, which makes it too slow to chase prey. Instead, when a fish comes close, it sends out a fleshy snout that is tipped with a venomous dart for harpooning its victim. The poison makes the fish go limp so the snail can swallow it whole.

### Dreadful dart

A cone snail waits for prey to come close before firing a poison dart. It will shoot at a careless human hand too, sometimes with fatal results.

Shiny, cone-shaped shell has a colorful pattern

Long, tubular mouthparts fire a poison dart into prey

## AT A GLANCE

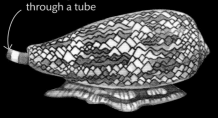

Snail senses prey by tasting the water through a tube

- **SIZE** ⅜–9 in (1–22 cm) shell length
- **HABITAT** Coastal ocean waters, often buried in sand
- **LOCATION** Warm and tropical oceans
- **DIET** Fish, worms, and other snails

## STATS AND FACTS

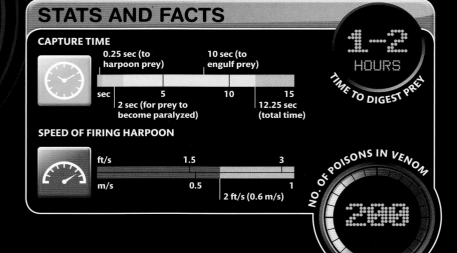

**CAPTURE TIME**

| | 0.25 sec (to harpoon prey) | | 10 sec (to engulf prey) | |
|---|---|---|---|---|
| sec | 5 | | 10 | 15 |
| | 2 sec (for prey to become paralyzed) | | | 12.25 sec (total time) |

**SPEED OF FIRING HARPOON**

| ft/s | | 1.5 | 3 |
|---|---|---|---|
| m/s | | 0.5 | 1 |
| | | 2 ft/s (0.6 m/s) | |

**1-2 HOURS** TIME TO DIGEST PREY

**NO. OF POISONS IN VENOM** 200

# OCEAN VAMPIRE
## SEA LAMPREY

The sea lamprey is a bloodthirsty animal, but it cannot bite because it has no jaws. Instead it has a mouth like a sucker, with teeth that rasp a wound into the flesh of other fish. It is a gory life for a fish that spends its early years in rivers as a tiny, harmless, wormlike larva. The larva grows by filtering plankton, before swimming into the sea and turning to meatier things.

Horny teeth around rim of mouth

"Tongue" also carries sharp teeth

### Jawless maw
A lamprey attacks anything big enough to take its weight. Its teeth hook onto the side of a fish. Then the mouth rasps away until it draws blood, swallowing the odd scale along the way.

## STATS AND FACTS

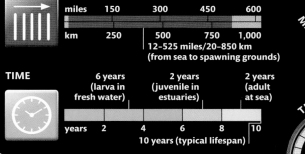

**MIGRATION DISTANCE**

| miles | 150 | 300 | 450 | 600 |
|---|---|---|---|---|
| km | 250 | 500 | 750 | 1,000 |

12–525 miles/20–850 km
(from sea to spawning grounds)

**TIME**

| | 6 years (larva in fresh water) | 2 years (juvenile in estuaries) | 2 years (adult at sea) |
|---|---|---|---|

| years | 2 | 4 | 6 | 8 | 10 |
|---|---|---|---|---|---|

10 years (typical lifespan)

**22 YEARS**
MAXIMUM LIFESPAN

**TEETH IN MOUTH**
**100**

# SPOTTED STINGER
## RIBBON-TAILED STINGRAY

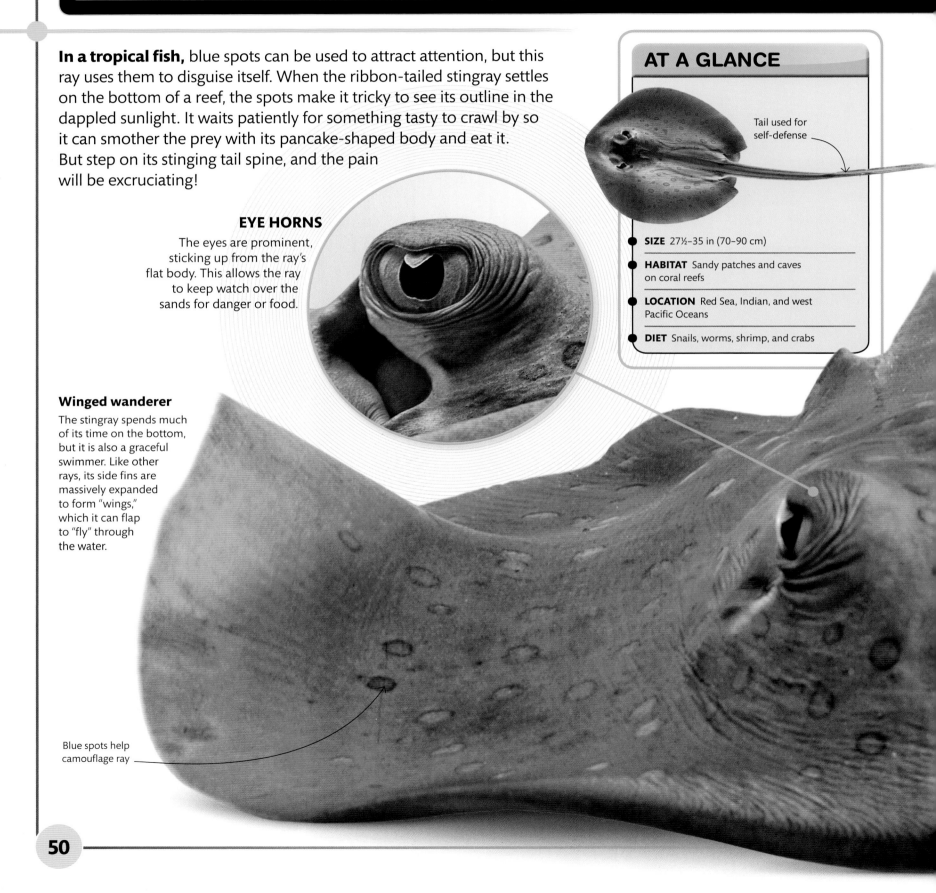

**In a tropical fish,** blue spots can be used to attract attention, but this ray uses them to disguise itself. When the ribbon-tailed stingray settles on the bottom of a reef, the spots make it tricky to see its outline in the dappled sunlight. It waits patiently for something tasty to crawl by so it can smother the prey with its pancake-shaped body and eat it. But step on its stinging tail spine, and the pain will be excruciating!

### EYE HORNS
The eyes are prominent, sticking up from the ray's flat body. This allows the ray to keep watch over the sands for danger or food.

### Winged wanderer
The stingray spends much of its time on the bottom, but it is also a graceful swimmer. Like other rays, its side fins are massively expanded to form "wings," which it can flap to "fly" through the water.

Blue spots help camouflage ray

## AT A GLANCE

Tail used for self-defense

- **SIZE** 27½–35 in (70–90 cm)
- **HABITAT** Sandy patches and caves on coral reefs
- **LOCATION** Red Sea, Indian, and west Pacific Oceans
- **DIET** Snails, worms, shrimp, and crabs

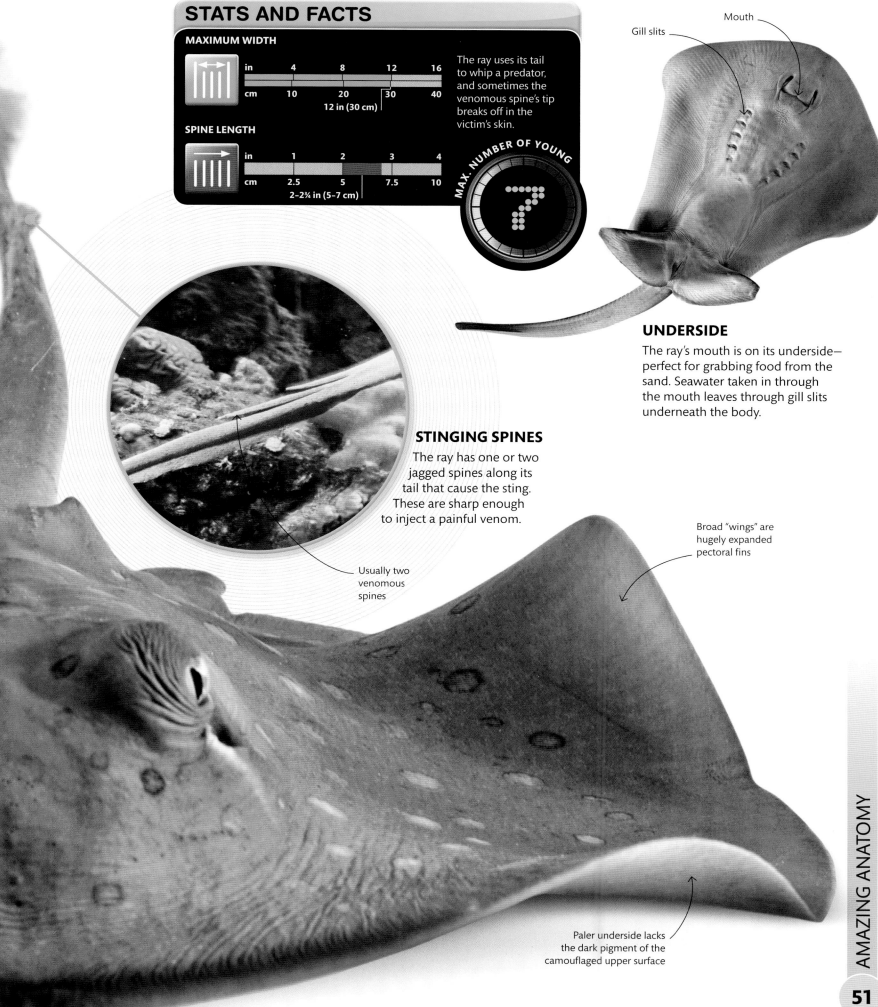

## STATS AND FACTS

**MAXIMUM WIDTH**

| in | 4 | 8 | 12 | 16 |
|---|---|---|---|---|
| cm | 10 | 20 | 30 | 40 |

12 in (30 cm)

The ray uses its tail to whip a predator, and sometimes the venomous spine's tip breaks off in the victim's skin.

**SPINE LENGTH**

| in | 1 | 2 | 3 | 4 |
|---|---|---|---|---|
| cm | 2.5 | 5 | 7.5 | 10 |

2-2¾ in (5-7 cm)

MAX. NUMBER OF YOUNG

**7**

Mouth

Gill slits

### UNDERSIDE

The ray's mouth is on its underside— perfect for grabbing food from the sand. Seawater taken in through the mouth leaves through gill slits underneath the body.

### STINGING SPINES

The ray has one or two jagged spines along its tail that cause the sting. These are sharp enough to inject a painful venom.

Usually two venomous spines

Broad "wings" are hugely expanded pectoral fins

Paler underside lacks the dark pigment of the camouflaged upper surface

# WALKING WONDER
## RED-LIPPED BATFISH

**No one knows for sure** why the red-lipped batfish wears so much face paint, but there is no mistaking how it gets its dinner. The batfish has a stubby fishing pole hidden under the "horn" on its forehead. When this pokes out, its tip releases a perfume into the water to entice prey. Although it is capable of swimming, this fish spends much of its time "walking" on the sea floor with stiffened leglike fins.

## AT A GLANCE

- **SIZE** 5½–8 in (14–20 cm) long
- **HABITAT** Tropical coastal waters on mud and sandy bottoms
- **LOCATION** Cocos and Galápagos Islands in the eastern Pacific Ocean
- **DIET** Small snails, clams, shrimp, worms, and fish

## STATS AND FACTS

**DEPTH**

| ft | 200 | 400 |
|---|---|---|
| m | 60 | 120 | 180 |

9¾–480 ft
(3–146 m)

**SPEED**

12 mph (20 km/h)
when swimming

| mph | 5 | 10 | 15 |
|---|---|---|---|
| km/h | 5 | 10 | 15 | 20 | 25 |

1¼ mph (2 km/h)
when walking

**SNOUT LENGTH**

| in | ⅛ | ¼ | ⅜ | ½ | ⅝ | ¾ |
|---|---|---|---|---|---|---|
| cm | 0.5 | 1 | 1.5 | 2 |

⅜ in (1 cm)

A batfish gets its name because its slow, crawling gait looks like that of a bat clambering over the ground. Batfish swim close to the ocean floor. Once settled on the seabed, their brown bodies are camouflaged as they clamber over sand and mud.

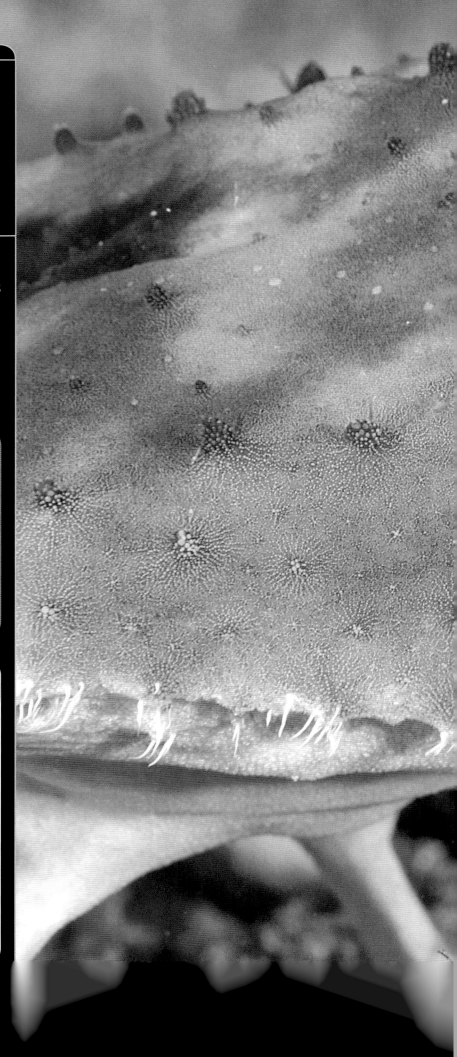

### CLOWN FACE

Thick red lips, a bristly beard, and a horn make a very bizarre underwater portrait, but this might help attract a mate. The red-lipped batfish is too slow to chase its food so it waits for prey to come close.

# DEADLY SUPERSTAR
## STARFISH

**Starfish look harmless but they hide a secret**—they are slow-moving hunters. Motionless mussels are perfect for them. A starfish pulls the shells apart with its arms and inserts its stomach to digest the victim alive. The starfish is not even bothered if it loses an arm through injury: it can simply grow a new one.

### Greedy guts

The starfish's mouth lies under its body. When feeding, it pushes its stomach out onto its prey and produces chemicals that start to digest the prey's body. The starfish then sucks up the juices.

Reproductive organs produce eggs or sperm

This species has five arms but others can have up to 50

## AT A GLANCE

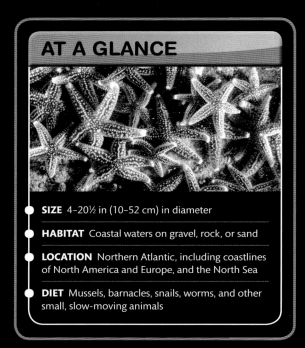

- **SIZE** 4–20½ in (10–52 cm) in diameter
- **HABITAT** Coastal waters on gravel, rock, or sand
- **LOCATION** Northern Atlantic, including coastlines of North America and Europe, and the North Sea
- **DIET** Mussels, barnacles, snails, worms, and other small, slow-moving animals

## STATS AND FACTS

**WALKING SPEED**

| | | | | 12 in (30 cm) per minute | |
|---|---|---|---|---|---|
| in/min | 3 | 6 | 9 | 12 | 15 |
| cm/min | 10 | 20 | 30 | 40 | |

**TIME**

| | | | 6–9 hours to open mussel | | |
|---|---|---|---|---|---|
| hrs | 2 | 4 | 6 | 8 | 10 |
| hrs | 2 | 4 | 6 | 8 | 10 |

2½–8 hours to digest mussel

**DISTANCE STOMACH EXTENDS**

| | in | ½ | 1 | 1½ | 2 |
|---|---|---|---|---|---|
| | cm | 1 | 2 | 3 | 4 | 5 |

¾–1½ in (2–4 cm)

**2.5 MILLION**
EGGS PER SPAWN

A starfish spends hours trying to pull open a mussel's shell until its victim tires and the starfish can get its stomach through the tiniest gap.

**TIME TO REGROW ARM**
**1 YEAR**

## INSIDE THE ARM

Each arm contains branches of the stomach for digestion and a system of tubes filled with seawater. The water carries nutrients and its pressure helps move the tiny tube feet.

Reproductive organ

Digestive gland

Tube foot

**CROSS SECTION ACROSS ARM**

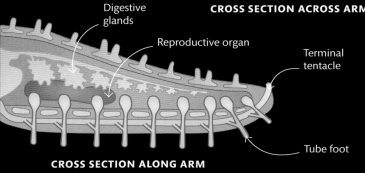

Digestive glands

Reproductive organ

Terminal tentacle

Tube foot

**CROSS SECTION ALONG ARM**

Each arm contains a complete set of reproductive organs, digestive glands, and a network of fluid-filled canals that move the tube feet

Rows of tube feet cover the underside of each foot

Tube feet are used for touching objects and walking

Stomach is a double-chambered sac in the middle of the animal that opens through the mouth on the lower surface and the anus on the upper surface

Madreporite is a tiny funnel that filters seawater into the body

### WALKING TUBE FEET

The underside of a starfish is covered in hundreds of tiny tube feet that work like miniature suckers. They help the animal crawl along and also provide a strong grip for pulling open mussels.

Water-filled tube encircles the central stomach and branches through each arm

Tiny water-filled sacs squeeze water into the tube feet to make them move

Digestive glands help break down food carried here from the stomach

Eyespots on the upper surface of each arm detect light

### ARMLESS TRICK

Each arm of a starfish contains a full set of the animal's main organ systems so a starfish can easily survive if it loses one of them. In any case, its powers of regeneration are so good that it can grow back a lost arm within a year.

## "A starfish can project its stomach through a 0.1 mm gap"

# NEVER-ENDING TENTACLES

## LION'S MANE JELLYFISH

**With more than a thousand** stinging tentacles—each growing longer than a bus—the lion's mane jellyfish is a giant of its kind. Its stingers leave whiplike scars on the skin and can even stop the heart. It swims by flapping its bell, while the deadly tentacles trail along behind, like a lion's mane. Those that get stranded on beaches are helpless—but their stings are still dangerous.

### AT A GLANCE

- **SIZE** Bell: 1–6½ ft (0.3–2 m) in diameter; tentacles: up to 121 ft (37 m) long

- **HABITAT** Open ocean

- **LOCATION** Northern Hemisphere, including North Atlantic and North Pacific Oceans, and North Sea

- **DIET** Fish, ragworms, and other small swimming animals

## STATS AND FACTS

**LENGTH**

65–98 ft/20–30 m (average)

| ft | 50 | 100 |
|---|---|---|

| m | 15 | 30 | 45 |
|---|---|---|---|

121 ft/37 m (maximum recorded length)

**WEIGHT**

136 lb/62 kg (human)

| lb | 1,000 | 2,000 |
|---|---|---|

| kg | 300 | 600 | 900 | 1,200 |
|---|---|---|---|---|

more than 2,200 lb/ 1,000 kg (jellyfish)

The tentacles of a lion's mane jellyfish are arranged in eight groups around a central mouth that hangs beneath the bell.

**MAX. NUMBER OF TENTACLES**

1,440

### ICE-COLD STINGER

The biggest lion's mane jellyfish live in the icy waters of the Arctic, where they usually swim near the surface. The bell varies in color, from blood-red to orange or yellow.

"A swarm of jellyfish can contain thousands of individuals"

AMAZING ANATOMY

# MONSTER MOUTH
## WHALE SHARK

**The huge whale shark** is really a gentle giant. It feeds on small fish and other animals floating in the plankton. Although it has a massive mouth, its throat is no wider than a man's arm. This prevents it from swallowing anything too big and ensures that the water sucked into its mouth passes out through its enormous gills instead. Anything edible is trapped by a special filter—so only food ends up going into its stomach.

### AT A GLANCE

- **SIZE** 52–66 ft (16–20 m)
- **HABITAT** Surface waters of the open ocean
- **LOCATION** Warm and tropical oceans around the world
- **DIET** Plankton (including krill—tiny, shrimplike animals), small fish, and squid

### STATS AND FACTS

**OVER 300 LITTER SIZE**

The whale shark spends most of its time cruising near the surface of the open ocean, where the plankton is most concentrated.

**GULPS PER MINUTE UP TO 28**

**WEIGHT**

| | 10 | 20 | 30 | 40 |
|---|---|---|---|---|
| tons | 10 | 20 | 30 | 40 |
| tonnes | 10 | 20 | 30 | 40 |

38 tons (34 tonnes)

**MIGRATION DISTANCE**

| | 2,000 | 4,000 | 6,000 | 8,000 |
|---|---|---|---|---|
| miles | 2,000 | 4,000 | 6,000 | 8,000 |
| km | 5,000 | 10,000 | 15,000 |

8,000 miles (13,000 km)

**SIZE OF PUPS**

| | 10 | 20 | 30 |
|---|---|---|---|
| in | 10 | 20 | 30 |
| cm | 20 | 40 | 60 | 80 |

16–23 in (40–60 cm)

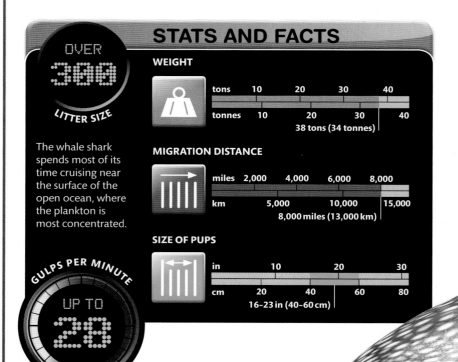

Pattern of white stripes and spots unlike any other shark

### Supersized shark

There are billions of tiny organisms living among the plankton, but it takes many mouthfuls to fill up this fish—even with a mouth 5 ft (1.5 m) wide. The whale shark consumes 2.2–3.3 tons (2–3 tonnes) of plankton a day. Second only to a whale in size, this is not only the largest shark but is also the biggest fish.

Whale sharks have around 4,000 small teeth, but they no longer have any useful function

Small eye on either side of mouth

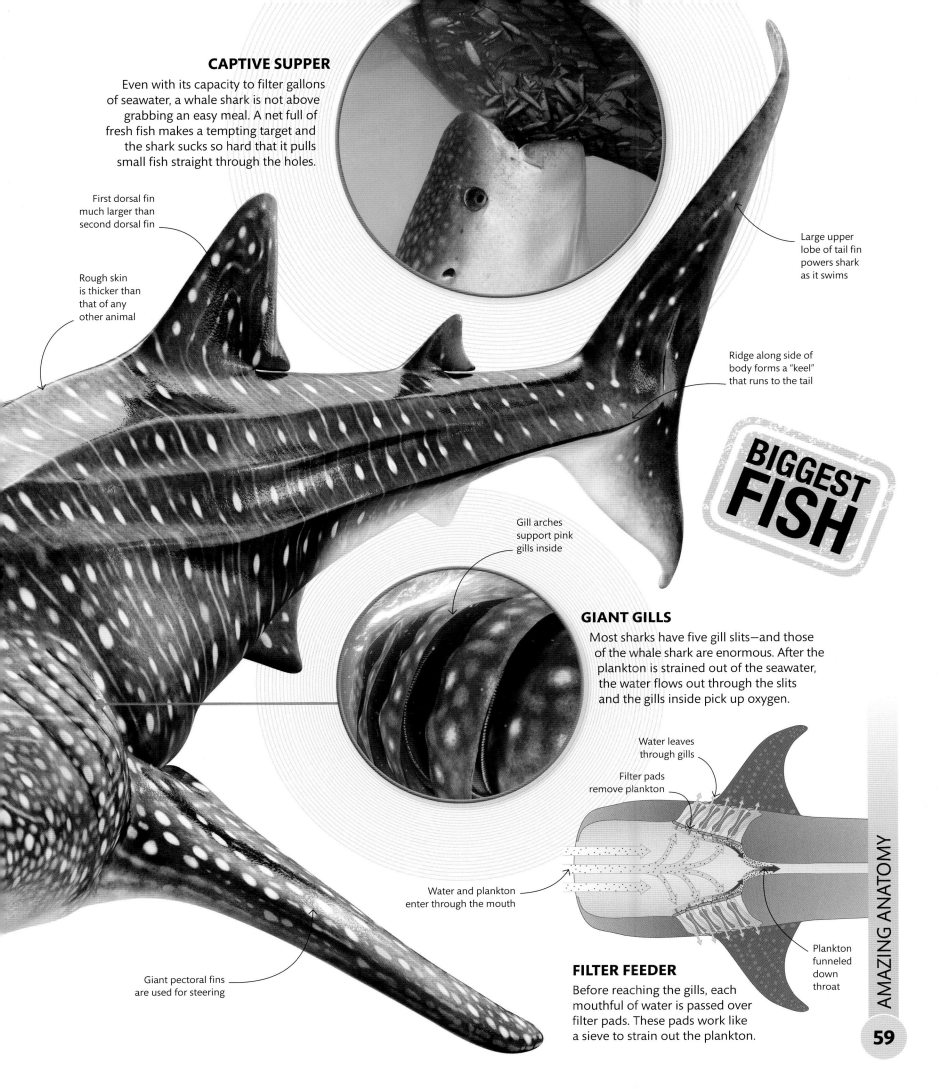

## CAPTIVE SUPPER

Even with its capacity to filter gallons of seawater, a whale shark is not above grabbing an easy meal. A net full of fresh fish makes a tempting target and the shark sucks so hard that it pulls small fish straight through the holes.

First dorsal fin much larger than second dorsal fin

Rough skin is thicker than that of any other animal

Large upper lobe of tail fin powers shark as it swims

Ridge along side of body forms a "keel" that runs to the tail

**BIGGEST FISH**

Gill arches support pink gills inside

## GIANT GILLS

Most sharks have five gill slits—and those of the whale shark are enormous. After the plankton is strained out of the seawater, the water flows out through the slits and the gills inside pick up oxygen.

Water leaves through gills

Filter pads remove plankton

Water and plankton enter through the mouth

Plankton funneled down throat

Giant pectoral fins are used for steering

## FILTER FEEDER

Before reaching the gills, each mouthful of water is passed over filter pads. These pads work like a sieve to strain out the plankton.

## SCHOOL SUCKER

Most of the ocean's filter-feeders get food by swimming forward with their mouth open, but the whale shark can strain food from seawater simply by gulping. When the shark opens its jaws wide, water rushes into its mouth at very high speed—pulling any small animals with it. In this way, hungry whale sharks can target entire schools of tiny fish, gobbling them down even when they're close to the surface.

LONGEST TEETH
RELATIVE
TO HEAD SIZE

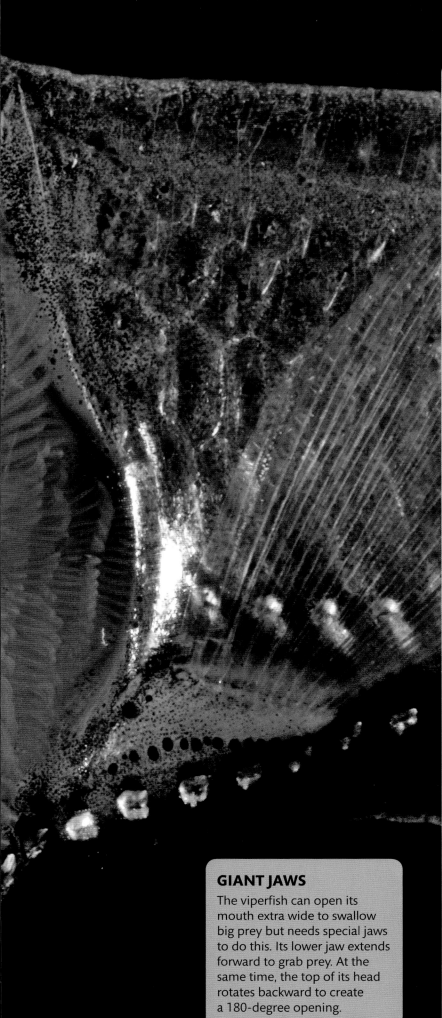

# FISHY FANGS
## SLOANE'S VIPERFISH

**The terrifying teeth of the deep-sea viperfish** are so long that they stick out when its mouth is closed. Food is scarce in the deepest ocean waters, so a predator needs clever tactics to get its meal. The viperfish has a flashing light at the end of a long spine on its back. This attracts the attention of other fish, and when they come close, the viperfish lunges with its fang-filled jaws. The bones behind its head are even specially strengthened to take the shock of the attack. It may take many days to make a kill, but the viperfish is patient and can go for a long time without eating anything at all.

## AT A GLANCE

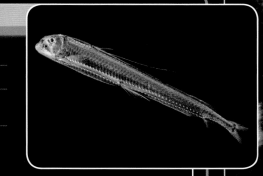

**SIZE** 8–14 in (20–35 cm) long

**HABITAT** Deep sea

**LOCATION** Tropical and subtropical oceans around the world

**DIET** Any animal that can fit into its mouth—mainly shrimp, squid, crabs, and small fish

## STATS AND FACTS

A viperfish moves slowly and spends a lot of time motionless in the water waiting for prey to come close enough for an attack.

**DEPTH**

1,605–3,280 ft/490–1,000 m (usual range)

| ft | 3,000 | 9,000 | 15,000 |
|---|---|---|---|
| m | 1,000 | 3,000 | 5,000 |

655–15,420 ft/ 200–4,700 m (total range)

**SWIMMING SPEED**

| mph | 0.5 | 1 |
|---|---|---|
| km/h | 1 | 2 |

less than 1 mph (1.5 km/h)

MAX. NUMBER OF TEETH
**26**

### GIANT JAWS
The viperfish can open its mouth extra wide to swallow big prey but needs special jaws to do this. Its lower jaw extends forward to grab prey. At the same time, the top of its head rotates backward to create a 180-degree opening.

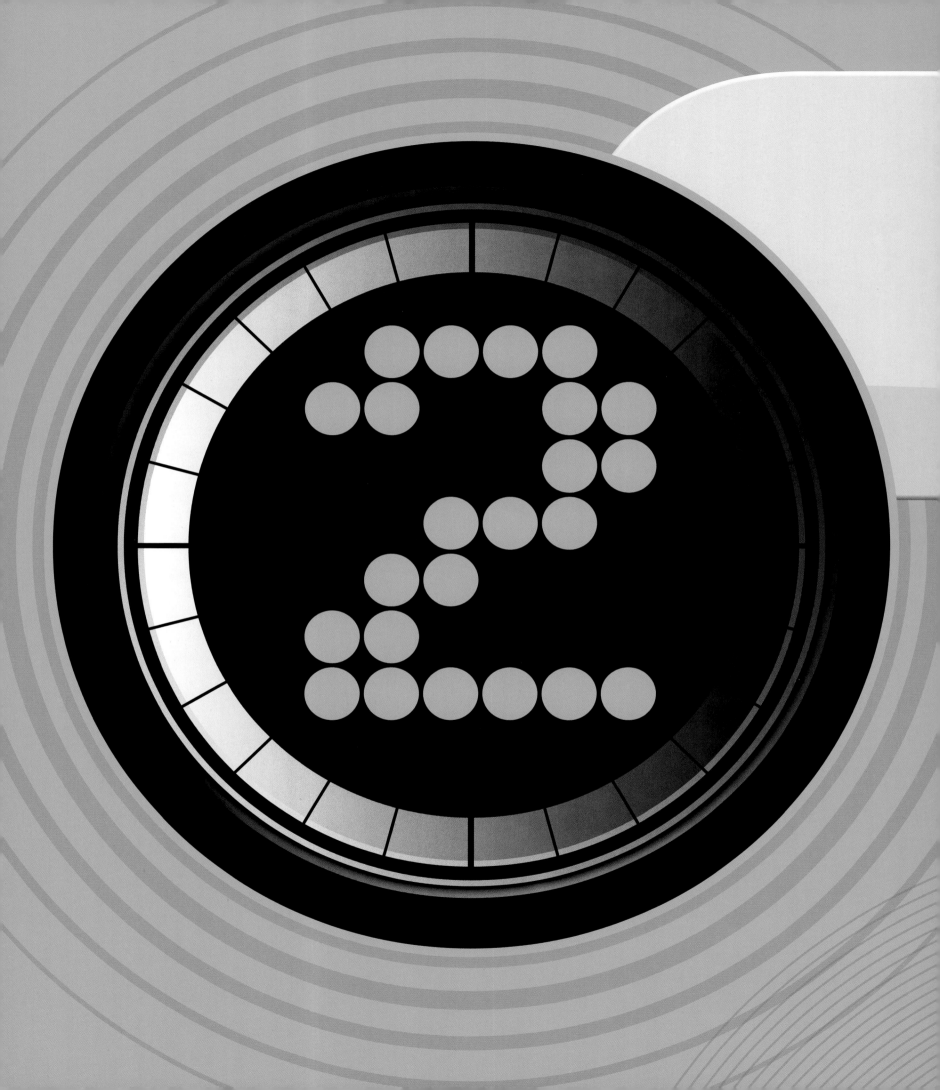

# ANIMAL ATHLETES

Some of the greatest athletes of the animal kingdom live in the sea. Only a cheetah can match the speed of a sailfish in pursuit of a meal, while very little escapes the enormous suction power of a nurse shark's mouth. And sometimes fish just want to have fun—jumping, spinning, and even flying high above the waves.

# OCEAN GLIDER
## FLYING FISH

**Oceans are filled with predators**, and sometimes there is only one thing a small fish can do to dodge danger: jump right out of the water. Flying fish do even better. They have winglike fins that take them farther through the air. With the help of breezes, they glide just above the surface and land with a splash many feet away. Most have two "wings" to carry them, but some species of flying fish have four and go longer distances. For the takeoff, the fish darts upward through the water and vibrates its tail with amazing speed, before spreading its "wings" to soar through the air.

## AT A GLANCE

- **SIZE** 7–20 in (18–50 cm) long
- **HABITAT** Surface waters of the open ocean
- **LOCATION** Worldwide; most abundant in the tropics
- **DIET** Plankton and small fish

Wings extend when gliding in air

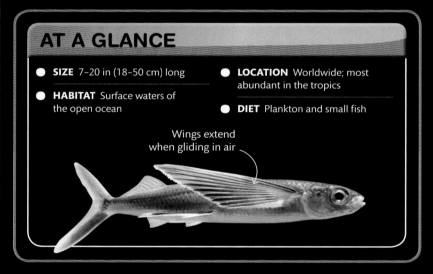

## STATS AND FACTS

**SPEED**

| mph | 15 | 30 | 45 |
|-----|----|----|----|
| km/h | 30 | 60 | 90 |

40 mph (64 km/h) while swimming | 43 mph (70 km/h) in flight

**45 SEC**
LONGEST FLIGHT

**HEIGHT REACHED**

| ft | 5 | 10 | 15 | 20 | 25 |
|----|---|----|----|----|----|
| m | 2 | 4 | 6 | 8 | |

20 ft (6 m) above water level

**78 PER SEC**
MAXIMUM TAIL BEATS

**SUPER GLIDER**
The long pectoral fins of a flying fish are high on the sides of the body and work just like the wings of a plane. It cannot flap its fins and so relies on gliding.

"Flying fish sometimes **land** on **boat decks**"

# JUMPING SHARK
## BLACKTIP SHARK

**This lively shark preys on big schools** of fish. It charges through them from below with such great speed that it jumps out of the water. Groups of blacktip sharks gather together to hunt and their excitement can build up into a feeding frenzy. As they attack, they twirl around in the water like a corkscrew, which continues into an acrobatic spin.

## AT A GLANCE

- **SIZE** 4¼–6½ ft (1.3–2 m) long
- **HABITAT** Oceans near continents and islands, including bays, river mouths, and coral reefs
- **LOCATION** Worldwide in warm and tropical ocean waters
- **DIET** Mainly fish, but also some shrimp, crabs, and squid

## STATS AND FACTS

**DEPTH**

| ft | | 40 | 80 |
|---|---|---|---|
| m | 15 | | 30 |

33 ft/10 m (starting depth before jump)

UP TO
**11**
PUPS PER LITTER

**JUMP HEIGHT**

| ft | | 2 | 4 |
|---|---|---|---|
| m | 0.5 | 1 | 1.5 |

1½–3¼ ft/0.5–1 m (approx.)

Some sharks jump from the water when they overshoot prey, but others do it to clear their body of parasites and other animals that might cling to their skin.

**JUMP SPEED**

| mph | 5 | 10 | 15 |
|---|---|---|---|
| km/h | 10 | 20 | 30 |

14 mph (23 km/h)

MAX. SPINS FROM WATER

**OCEANS OF FOOD**

Fish sometimes gather in schools to make it difficult for predators to focus on a single target, but that doesn't deter blacktip sharks. Instead, they dive speedily through the schools, snapping as they go.

# SPEEDIEST SWIMMER

## SAILFISH

**Nothing in the ocean can match the speed** of a sailfish. As it darts around the water, its body flashes blue or yellow, which helps confuse its prey of smaller schooling fish and squid. When it gets especially excited, the sailfish even raises its massive dorsal fin like a sail on its back.

> "Its body can rapidly change color to show its mood"

### Built for speed

The sailfish's streamlined body helps it cut through the water with ease. Its muscles are blood-red because they contain a red pigment that stores the oxygen needed to provide bursts of energy. These muscles generate heat, which also helps them work at peak performance.

Long pointed bill used to jab and slash at schools of fish

Heat produced by the eye muscles keeps its eyes warm and may help it see in dim light

Massive sail-like fin runs down most of body

**HERDING SCHOOLS**

Sailfish usually keep their sails flat against the body when they are in mid-chase, but they can pull them up as a way of scaring schools of fish into tighter bunches, before attacking with their sharp bills.

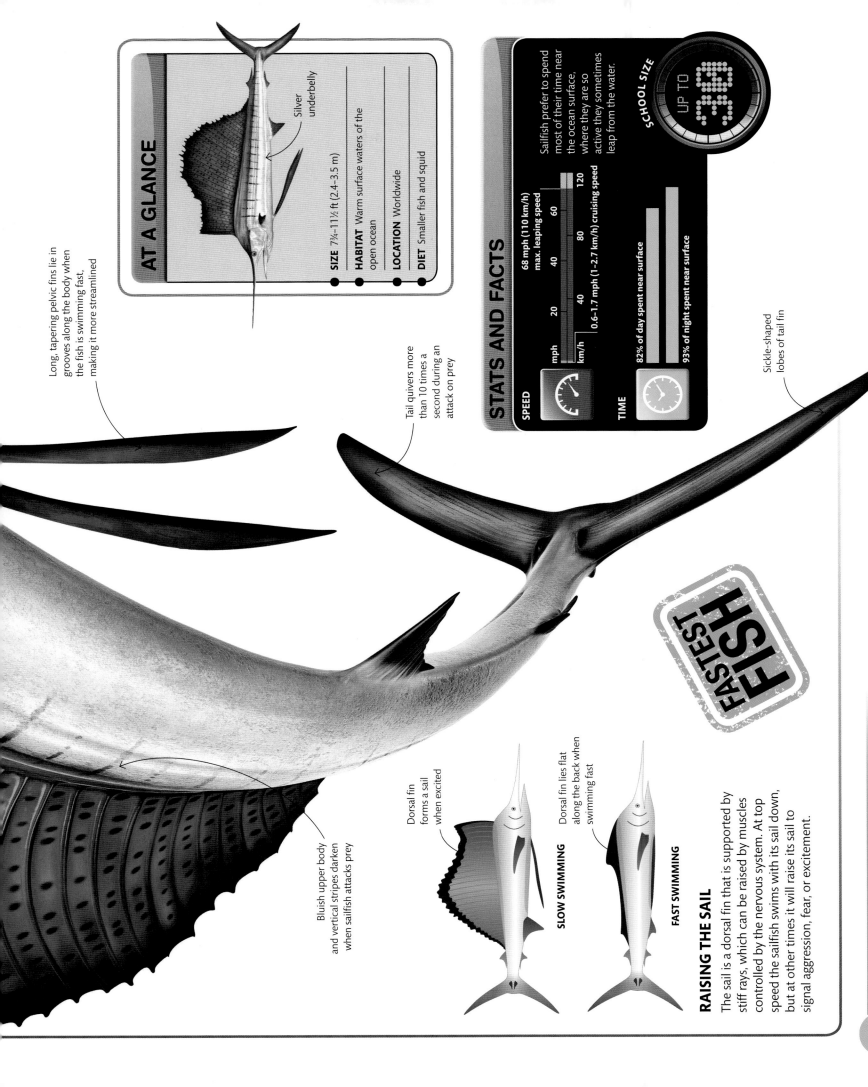

## AT A GLANCE

Silver underbelly

**SIZE** 7¾–11½ ft (2.4–3.5 m)

**HABITAT** Warm surface waters of the open ocean

**LOCATION** Worldwide

**DIET** Smaller fish and squid

Long, tapering pelvic fins lie in grooves along the body when the fish is swimming fast, making it more streamlined

Tail quivers more than 10 times a second during an attack on prey

## STATS AND FACTS

Sailfish prefer to spend most of their time near the ocean surface, where they are so active they sometimes leap from the water.

**SPEED**

68 mph (110 km/h) max. leaping speed

mph 20 40 60
km/h 40 80 120 0.6–1.7 mph (1–2.7 km/h) cruising speed

**TIME**

82% of day spent near surface

93% of night spent near surface

**SCHOOL SIZE** UP TO 8

Bluish upper body and vertical stripes darken when sailfish attacks prey

Sickle-shaped lobes of tail fin

**FASTEST FISH**

Dorsal fin forms a sail when excited

**SLOW SWIMMING**

Dorsal fin lies flat along the back when swimming fast

**FAST SWIMMING**

### RAISING THE SAIL

The sail is a dorsal fin that is supported by stiff rays, which can be raised by muscles controlled by the nervous system. At top speed the sailfish swims with its sail down, but at other times it will raise its sail to signal aggression, fear, or excitement.

### SUCKER FISH

This nurse shark carries a hitchhiking remora. This is a smaller fish that has a head-sucker so it can attach to the shark and enjoy a free ride. It might also get any scraps of food the shark drops.

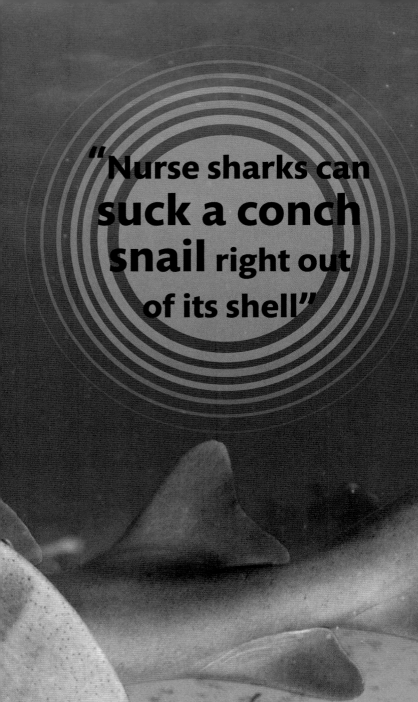

"Nurse sharks can **suck a conch snail** right out of its shell"

# FASTEST MOUTH
## NURSE SHARK

**The gummy-looking mouth** of a nurse shark doesn't look very threatening, but this fish relies on suction rather than biting. It inflates its throat so much—and opens its mouth so quickly—that any little fish or crab in its path is sucked inside before it has a chance to get away. The loud sucking noise it makes sounds like a nursing baby, and may have given this shark its name. Its teeth are small but sharply pointed, so it can chomp through anything that reaches its jaws. Nurse sharks patrol shallow coastlines mainly at night. By day they like the safety of each other's company and spend their time resting together in dark caves, where they are often found piled one on top of another.

### AT A GLANCE

**SIZE** 7¼–14 ft (2.25–4.3 m)

**HABITAT** Coastal waters on rocky reefs, over sand flats, and near mangroves

**LOCATION** Atlantic, Caribbean, and Eastern Pacific coastlines, especially near the equator

**DIET** Bottom-living invertebrates (such as snails, squid, and crabs) and fish, hunted at night

### STATS AND FACTS

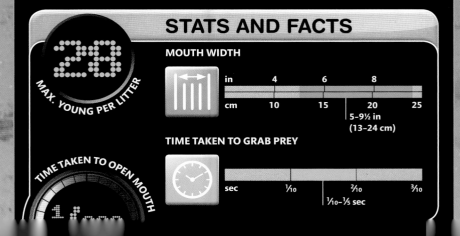

**28** MAX. YOUNG PER LITTER

**MOUTH WIDTH**

| in | | 4 | 6 | 8 | |
|---|---|---|---|---|---|
| cm | 10 | 15 | 20 | | 25 |

5–9½ in
(13–24 cm)

**TIME TAKEN TO GRAB PREY**

| sec | ¹⁄₁₀ | ²⁄₁₀ | ³⁄₁₀ |
|---|---|---|---|

¹⁄₁₀–¹⁄₅ sec

TIME TAKEN TO OPEN MOUTH

## HUNGRY VACUUM

A nurse shark is not as ferocious as many biting sharks, but it has the right equipment to be a champion sucker. It has a small mouth that faces forward rather than downward. When it spots something, it lowers its head toward the prey. Then, in the blink of an eye, it drops its bottom jaw and purses its strong lips to form a round tube. With a sudden, sharp gulp, the prey is sucked up into the mouth.

**LIVING POM-POMS**

Many other crabs have chunky pincers, but the boxer crab has slender fingerlike pincers for holding its precious anemones. Should it lose one anemone, it will carefully tear the other in two to make a replacement.

# PUT 'EM UP!

## BOXER CRAB

**Here is a crab that is no bigger** than your thumbnail, but what it lacks in size it makes up for in nerve. It clasps a miniature stinging anemone in each pincer and holds them out like a pair of pom-poms or boxing gloves. Should any predator come too close, the boxer crab waves the anemones about, and the stings help keep the danger away. But carrying anemones also has its problems. The crab cannot use its pincers to break up food. Instead it nibbles on plankton that sticks to the anemone's tentacles. When two boxer crabs meet, each makes a show of waving their pom-poms in a pretend fight, but they rarely make physical contact.

### AT A GLANCE

- **SIZE** ⅜–1 in (1–2.5 cm) shell width
- **HABITAT** Coral reefs
- **LOCATION** Tropical coastlines
- **DIET** Tiny animal plankton, collected with its anemone pom-poms

"Some boxer crabs use their anemones to **brush food off rocks**"

### STATS AND FACTS

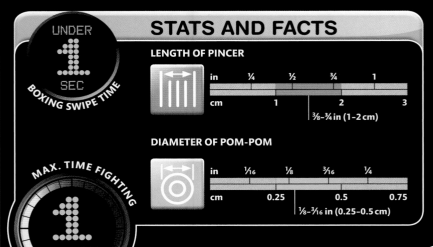

UNDER **1** SEC
BOXING SWIPE TIME

**LENGTH OF PINCER**

| in | ¼ | ½ | ¾ | 1 |
|---|---|---|---|---|
| cm | | 1 | 2 | 3 |

⅜–¾ in (1–2 cm)

MAX. TIME FIGHTING
**1** MINUTE

**DIAMETER OF POM-POM**

| in | 1⁄16 | ⅛ | 3⁄16 | ¼ |
|---|---|---|---|---|
| cm | 0.25 | | 0.5 | 0.75 |

⅛–3⁄16 in (0.25–0.5 cm)

**A SHOCKING TAIL**

The thresher shark hunts fish and hits them with its long tail. Some are killed by a direct hit, but others are left stunned by the shock of the whip.

"The **force** of the **tail whip** is so great that it **boils the water** at the tail's tip"

# LASHING OUT
## THRESHER SHARK

**No other shark hunts** quite like the thresher shark. Its tail is as long as its entire body, and is used like a whip to stun prey. Thresher sharks chase around in the open ocean and, like their bigger cousin the great white shark, they can stay active because their blood is warmer than the surroundings. Once they find a school of fish, they circle it to bunch their prey closer together. Then they smack their tails so fast that the shock alone leaves prey floating and ready to eat.

## AT A GLANCE

- **SIZE** 12½–25 ft (3.8–7.6 m) long
- **HABITAT** Open ocean waters, especially near continents
- **LOCATION** Worldwide
- **DIET** Mainly schooling fish, such as mackerel, but also squid

## STATS AND FACTS

A thresher's tail is so long that it can reach forward and whip at prey over the top of the shark's head. Pairs or small groups may hunt together and, like some other kinds of energetic sharks, they often jump out of the water.

**WEIGHT**

| | lb | 400 | 800 | 1,200 |
|---|---|---|---|---|
| | kg | 200 | 400 | 600 |

167–350 lb/
76–160 kg
(tail weight)

500–1,125 lb/
230–510 kg
(total weight)

**TAIL LENGTH**

| | ft | | 5 | | 10 | |
|---|---|---|---|---|---|---|
| | m | 1 | 2 | 3 | | 4 |

6½–12 ft
(2–3.8 m)

**SPEED OF TAIL WHIP**

| | mph | 30 | 60 | 90 |
|---|---|---|---|---|
| | km/h | 50 | 100 | 150 |

31–80 mph
(50–130 km/h)

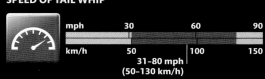

**LIFESPAN**

# LONGEST
## TAIL COMPARED TO BODY SIZE

# WHIRLING WONDER
## SPINNER DOLPHIN

**Dolphins and whales** are famous for their playful acrobatics in the ocean. The spinner dolphin is one of the most agile and gets its name from its twisting leaps. It shoots up through the water like a corkscrew, so that when it breaks clear of the surface, it spins in the air. Some dolphins are so eager that they do this many times in succession.

### AT A GLANCE

- **SIZE** 4¼–7½ ft (1.3–2.3 m) long

- **HABITAT** Warm ocean waters, usually near coastlines but sometimes on the high seas hundreds of miles from land

- **LOCATION** Throughout the tropical parts of the world's oceans

- **DIET** Fish, squid, and shrimp, mostly taken at night

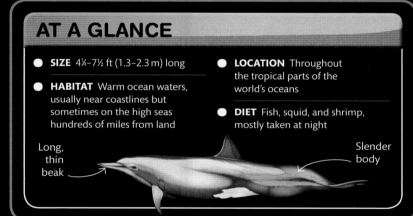

Long, thin beak

Slender body

### STATS AND FACTS

**1.25 SEC**

TIME SPENT IN AIR

Spinning leaps may help dolphins socialize in their groups. They could also be a way of removing clinging barnacles from their bodies.

MAX. ROTATIONS PER LEAP

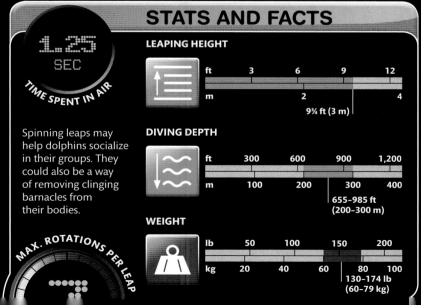

**LEAPING HEIGHT**

| | ft | 3 | 6 | 9 | 12 |
|---|---|---|---|---|---|
| | m | | 2 | | 4 |

9¾ ft (3 m)

**DIVING DEPTH**

| | ft | 300 | 600 | 900 | 1,200 |
|---|---|---|---|---|---|
| | m | 100 | 200 | 300 | 400 |

655–985 ft (200–300 m)

**WEIGHT**

| | lb | 50 | 100 | 150 | 200 |
|---|---|---|---|---|---|
| | kg | 20 | 40 | 60 | 80 | 100 |

130–174 lb (60–79 kg)

### SPIN ON THE SEA

When spinner dolphins get together in groups they like nothing better than to show off. They make spinning leaps headfirst from the water and

# BUILT FOR SPEED
## SHORTFIN MAKO

**Meet the champion swimmer** of the shark world. The shortfin mako is the fastest shark over long distances and is perfectly capable of catching fast-swimming prey, such as tuna and swordfish. When it's in mid-chase it can make sharp turns in the water, too. All this frantic activity generates a lot of heat in its muscles. Much of this heat is trapped within the body, so the shark is effectively warm-blooded. The shortfin mako lives in the open ocean, but it migrates to tropical waters during the winter months to help keep its body warm.

## AT A GLANCE

- **SIZE** 10½–13 ft (3.2–4 m)
- **HABITAT** Warm and tropical coastal ocean waters, mainly deep water
- **LOCATION** Worldwide near coastlines
- **DIET** Mainly fish and squid, but sometimes sea turtles and dolphins

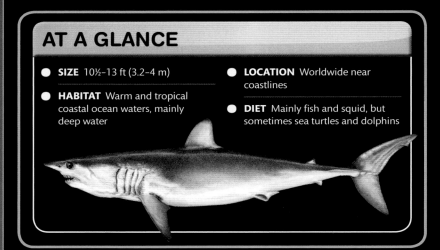

## STATS AND FACTS

**SPEED**

0.8–1.7 mph (1.3–2.8 km/h) cruising speed

| mph | 15 | 30 | 45 |
| --- | --- | --- | --- |
| km/h | 25 | 50 | 75 |

46 mph (74 km/h) in max. burst

**32 YEARS** MAX. LIFESPAN

**DISTANCE TRAVELED**

2,130 miles/3,430 km (max. migration)

| miles | 500 | 1,000 | 1,500 | 2,000 |
| --- | --- | --- | --- | --- |
| km | 1,000 | 2,000 | 3,000 | 4,000 |

36 miles/58 km (average per day)

**TIME TO DIGEST MEAL**

**2 DAYS**

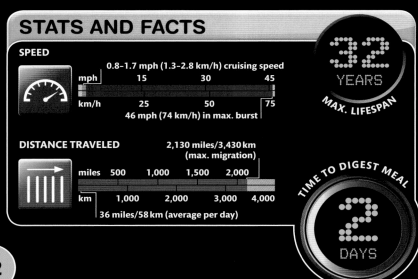

FASTEST SHARK

> "The horns on the ray's head are **fins** that **funnel food** towards its mouth"

# FANTASTIC FLYER
## MOBULA RAY

**When a school of mobula rays** puts on a show it is one of the greatest natural wonders of the ocean. Hundreds can jump from the water, flapping their "wings" and doing somersaults. These acrobatics may be to show off to each other or a way to dislodge parasites. It is also possible that they are playing so quickly near the ocean surface that they become airborne by accident.

### AT A GLANCE

- **SIZE** 3–21 ft (0.9 –6.5 m) length including tail; 17 ft (5.2 m) disk width
- **HABITAT** Warm and tropical ocean waters near coastlines
- **LOCATION** Worldwide
- **DIET** Plankton, small crustaceans, and small fish filtered from the water

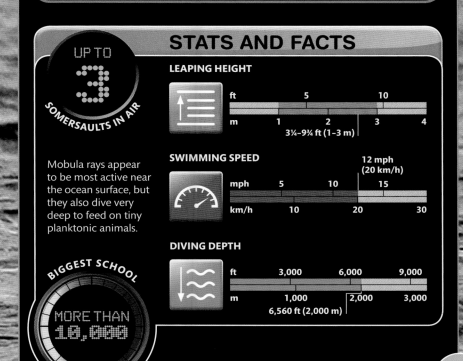

### STATS AND FACTS

UP TO
**3**
SOMERSAULTS IN AIR

Mobula rays appear to be most active near the ocean surface, but they also dive very deep to feed on tiny planktonic animals.

BIGGEST SCHOOL
MORE THAN
**10,000**

**LEAPING HEIGHT**

| ft | | 5 | | 10 | |
|---|---|---|---|---|---|
| m | 1 | 2 | 3 | 4 |

3¼–9¾ ft (1–3 m)

**SWIMMING SPEED**

12 mph (20 km/h)

| mph | 5 | 10 | 15 | |
|---|---|---|---|---|
| km/h | 10 | 20 | 30 |

**DIVING DEPTH**

| ft | 3,000 | 6,000 | 9,000 |
|---|---|---|---|
| m | 1,000 | 2,000 | 3,000 |

6,560 ft (2,000 m)

### SPLASHING SPECTACLE

A display of leaping mobula rays is an energetic and noisy spectacle. A group of rays may jump several times in succession, landing in the water with a big splash each time.

# SCHOOL CHASER
## BRONZE WHALER

**A giant school of little fish** can sometimes satisfy the appetite of the biggest sharks. Bronze whalers get their name from their coppery color and the fact that they have been seen snacking on dead whales. These sharks cannot resist the annual migration of sardines that moves along the South African coast. Bronze whalers are the most common sharks to be drawn to the spectacle, and arrive in large numbers, with each shark diving deep into the school to feast on the tightly packed bundles of prey.

## AT A GLANCE

- **SIZE** 7¾–9½ ft (2.4 m–2.9 m) long

- **HABITAT** Warm and subtropical ocean waters, mainly near coastlines; it also enters estuaries and lower reaches of some rivers

- **LOCATION** Warm coastlines of all oceans and the Mediterranean Sea

- **DIET** Fish, stingrays, spiny dogfish, squid, cuttlefish, and octopuses

## STATS AND FACTS

**ACTIVITY**

Females and young most active (during sardine run in June–July)    Males active all year around

January    December

**DIET**

Other prey 35%

Sardines 48%    Cuttlefish 17%

**MATURITY AGE**

13 years (male)

20 years (female)

Sardines follow currents of cool water when they migrate during the southern winter months of June and July. The migration entices many bronze whalers, including females and young that have been spending their time in shallower nursery waters.

## FISHY FEAST

The bronze whaler snags mouthfuls of sardines with its sharply pointed teeth. There are so many of the little fish that even when large groups of

## A QUICK LANDING

Gentoo penguins swim so fast they shoot straight out of the water before coming in to land. Speed is not only important for catching prey but also for avoiding predators, such as leopard seals.

# "Gentoo penguins can travel 16 miles (26 km) from land during their fishing expeditions"

## DAPPER DIVER
### GENTOO PENGUIN

**Short legs, big feet**, and an upright body make penguins look comical on land. Even when they are in a hurry, a waddle or belly-slide is the best they can do. But in the water they turn into graceful swimmers and gentoo penguins are the fastest of the lot. They dive into the ocean hundreds of times every day, launching themselves from slippery packs of floating ice and slicing cleanly through the waves. Once underwater, their streamlined bodies and flipperlike wings help them reach speeds of up to 22 mph (36 km/h) to catch fish and other prey—faster than most other kinds of diving birds.

### AT A GLANCE

- **SIZE** 30–32 in (76–81 cm) body length
- **HABITAT** Rocky coastlines and adjoining seas
- **LOCATION** Islands around Antarctica
- **DIET** Krill, fish, worms, and squid

**FASTEST PENGUIN UNDERWATER**

### STATS AND FACTS

UP TO
**24**
DIVES PER HOUR

DIVE DURATION
**86** SEC

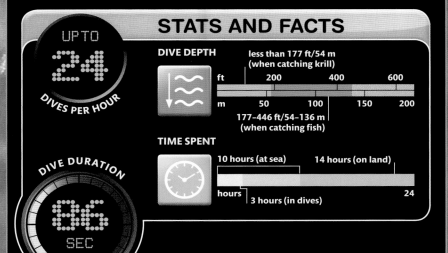

**DIVE DEPTH**

less than 177 ft/54 m (when catching krill)

| ft | 200 | 400 | 600 |
|---|---|---|---|
| m | 50 | 100 | 150 | 200 |

177–446 ft/54–136 m (when catching fish)

**TIME SPENT**

| hours | 10 hours (at sea) | 14 hours (on land) |
|---|---|---|

3 hours (in dives)                          24

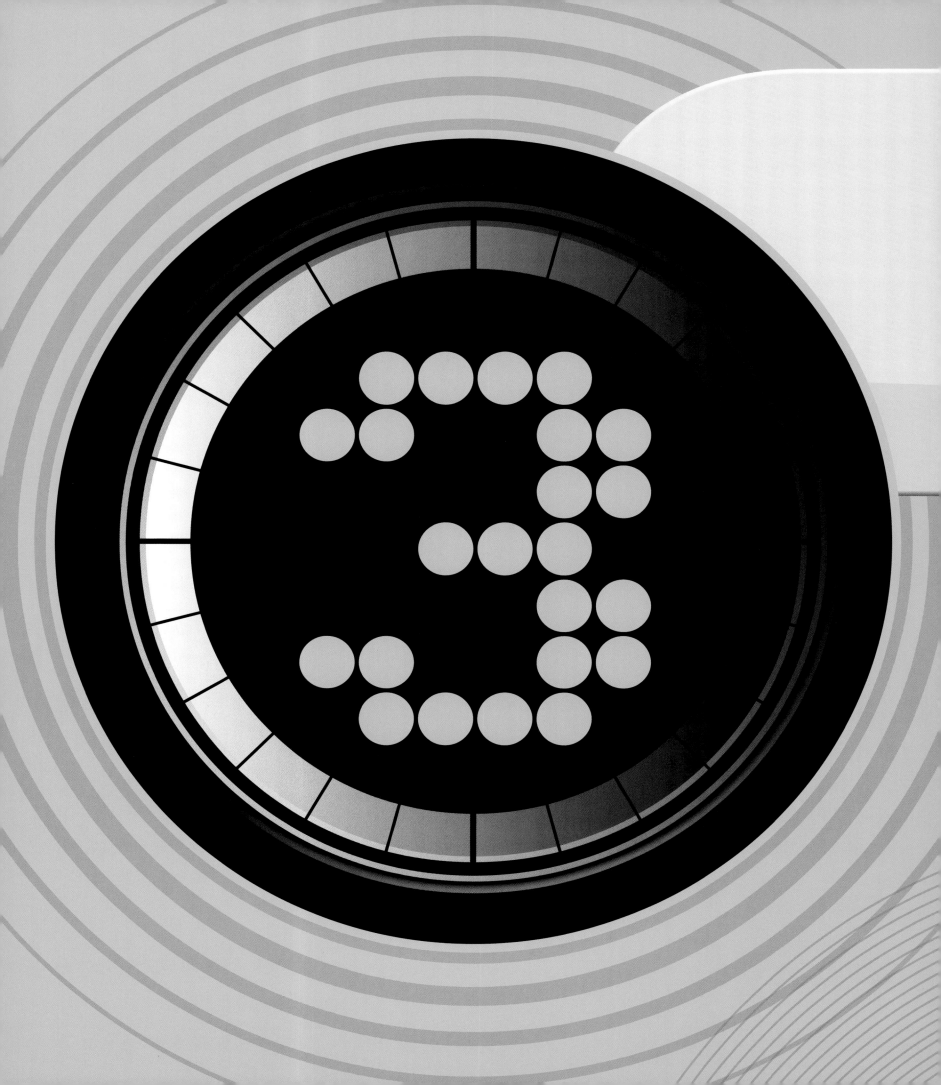

# LIFE STORIES

Life in the ocean is tough—it can be cold, dark, and hard to find anything to eat or anywhere to hide. To improve its chances of survival, an animal needs to develop a special skill or way of living that makes the most of its environment and protects it from predators.

**PORTABLE NURSERY**

Male jawfishes have a bigger mouth than females because only males brood the eggs. There must be enough room inside their mouth to let water flow around the eggs and give them enough oxygen.

# MALE MOUTHBROODER
## JAWFISH

**It looks like a tight squeeze** but what better place for baby jawfishes to hide from danger than in their dad's mouth? He scoops up a hundred or so of his partner's eggs in his mouth and cares for them as they develop. Once hatched, he will spit them into the ocean current and his work is done. Then he will return to using his big mouth for shifting sand and stones. In this way he can keep his burrow in order and make sure that it does not cave in. He selects stones and pieces of rock that are just right for reinforcing the sides of his burrow.

## AT A GLANCE

- **SIZE** 1½–20 in (4–50 cm) long
- **HABITAT** Shallow marine coastal waters, where they burrow in sand or silt
- **LOCATION** Western Atlantic, Indian, and Pacific Oceans
- **DIET** Small animals caught on the sea floor or from the plankton

## STATS AND FACTS

Jawfish use their big mouths to dig burrows. Some even prop a stone "door" at the entrance for extra protection.

**GAPE OF MOUTH**

| in | | 1 | | 2 | | 3 |
|----|---|---|---|---|---|---|
| cm | 2 | | 4 | 6 | | 8 |

approx. ³⁄₁₆–2½ in
(0.5–6.5 cm)

**DEPTH OF BURROW**

| in | | 10 | | 20 | |
|----|---|----|---|----|---|
| cm | 20 | | 40 | | 60 |

approx. 4–20 in
(10–50 cm)

TIME FOR EGGS TO HATCH

7–10 DAYS

# COY CURLER
## SHY SHARK

**There are certain advantages** to being a small shark—it is easier to reach tasty worms and fish among the rocks and coral along coastal shallows. However, it makes you a target for fiercer predators, so it helps if you have a strategy for keeping out of their way. Shy sharks certainly live up to their name. They hide to avoid being grabbed by sea lions diving from the shore or bigger sharks coming up from the deep. As a last resort, shy sharks curl themselves into a ring when a danger threatens. A ring shape makes a tricky mouthful for a hungry predator to gulp down.

## AT A GLANCE

- **SIZE** 19½–29 in (50–73 cm) long
- **HABITAT** Mainly shallow ocean waters with rocky and sandy bottoms or over beds of kelp
- **LOCATION** Southern Africa
- **DIET** Small fish, worms, shrimp, crabs, and squid

## STATS AND FACTS

**SWIMMING DEPTH**

| ft | 150 | 300 | 450 |
|----|-----|-----|-----|
| m | 50 | 100 | 150 |

0–426 ft (0–130 m)

Unlike most other sharks, shy sharks do not give birth to live young. The pups hatch from egg cases that are laid in shallow waters.

**LENGTH**

4–4¼ in (10–11 cm)
size of pups at hatching

| in | 10 | 20 | |
|----|-----|-----|-----|
| cm | 25 | 50 | 75 |

19½–29 in (50–73 cm)
size of adults

TIME FOR EGGS TO HATCH
**14 WEEKS**

94

"The biggest **sardine schools** are **so large** they are visible by **satellite**"

# SUPER-SIZED SCHOOL

## SARDINE

**Some kinds of fish** love to get together, and when sardines assemble they make some of the biggest schools of all. Each year, billions of them follow the cool ocean currents that stream up the east coast of Africa, making such a spectacle that the event is called the sardine run. The total weight of moving animals might be the heaviest migration on the planet. Sardines are small fish of the herring family that find safety in numbers. A big school might look like easy pickings, but a predator will find it difficult to focus on a single moving target among the silver, shimmering mass of fish.

## AT A GLANCE

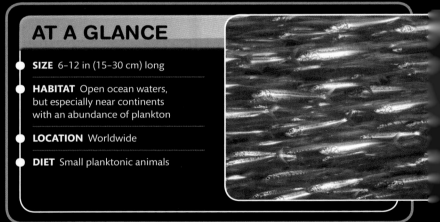

- **SIZE** 6–12 in (15–30 cm) long

- **HABITAT** Open ocean waters, but especially near continents with an abundance of plankton

- **LOCATION** Worldwide

- **DIET** Small planktonic animals

## STATS AND FACTS

No one is sure why a giant sardine run comes together to school, but some think it is triggered by yearly changes in the ocean currents.

**EST. SCHOOL SIZE**

**18**

**LENGTH OF A GIANT SCHOOL**

| miles | 5 | 10 | 15 |
|---|---|---|---|
| km | 10 | 20 | 30 |

9 miles (15 km)

**DEPTH OF A GIANT SCHOOL**

| ft | 50 | 100 | 150 |
|---|---|---|---|
| m | 20 | 40 | 60 |

98 ft (30 m)

### SCHOOLING TOGETHER

A massive school of sardines moves about like a single gigantic living thing. A single fish is safer mixed among lots of others, and by streaming together it might take less

# REPTILE ON THE ROCKS
## MARINE IGUANA

**Lizards usually keep their feet firmly on dry land,** but here is one that is not afraid of getting them wet. On the rocky shores of the Galápagos Islands, off South America, the marine iguana eats nothing but seaweed. Some of this grows above the shoreline, but a large iguana must take a dip into the ocean to really satisfy its appetite.

### SEAWEED SNACK

The marine iguana has a blunt snout so it can get its sharp teeth really close to the rocks where seaweed grows. It will nibble green seaweed, but prefers a red type that mainly grows under water.

## STATS AND FACTS

Like all reptiles, a marine iguana relies on sunshine to warm its body and stay active. When it dives into the cold ocean, its body temperature falls, so it cannot stay there for long. Only big iguanas make dives because smaller ones lose heat too quickly.

**TEMPERATURE**

52–73°F/11–23°C
(temperature of seawater)

| °F | 50 | 75 | 100 |
|---|---|---|---|

| °C | 15 | 30 | 45 |
|---|---|---|---|

95–102°F/35–39°C (body temperature when active)

**DIVING DEPTH**

66 ft/20 m (maximum)

| ft | 20 | 40 | 60 | 80 |
|---|---|---|---|---|

| m | 5 | 10 | 15 | 20 | 25 |
|---|---|---|---|---|---|

**DIET**

95% of seaweed grazed above sea surface

5% of seaweed grazed below sea surface

**MAX. DIVE DURATION**

**60 MINS**

Skin is largely gray or black, but in the breeding season it develops pink or green patches, which may flush a deeper color

Ragged "fin" running along the back and tail helps control position while swimming

Long, side-flattened tail helps provide propulsion when swimming

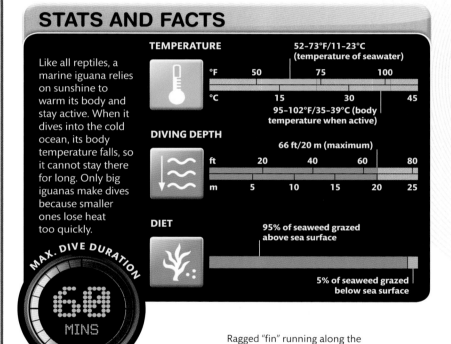

Iguanas use their stocky heads to butt rivals and may even deliberately sneeze over one another

**Super sunbather**

The dark skin of a marine iguana soaks up the Sun's rays and helps warm it up. The color, pattern, and size of iguanas varies from island to island. Males are more brightly colored than females.

## AT A GLANCE

**SIZE** 3¼–5½ ft (1–1.7 m) long

**HABITAT** Rocky shores

**LOCATION** Galápagos Islands

**DIET** Seaweed

Strong jaws contain sharp, three-pronged teeth for pulling on seaweed

Salt gland above eye drains into nostril

Face is often encrusted with white patches of salt sneezed out through the nostrils

### SALT SNEEZER

Seaweed is so salty the iguana needs special glands in its head to remove extra salt from its blood and stop it from building up. The iguana snorts to clear the salty snot out of its nose.

Sharp claws help grip rocks, especially when the lizard is battered by waves

# A HOME WITH A STING
## CLOWNFISH

**Some animals do strange things** to stay safe on an ocean reef filled with predators. For a clownfish family this means snuggling down among the tentacles of an anemone. The tentacles have stingers, but a clownfish is not bothered by them and never swims very far from their reach. In fact, both anemone and clownfish benefit from living together. The clownfish is protected from bigger predators that stay away because they can get stung, and the anemone gets the odd morsel of food dropped when the clownfish grabs a meal from the floating plankton.

## AT A GLANCE

- **SIZE** 2–5 in (5–13 cm)
- **HABITAT** On tropical coral reefs, in and around sea anemones
- **LOCATION** Coastal waters of eastern Indian Ocean and western Pacific Ocean
- **DIET** Plankton and dead scraps

## STATS AND FACTS

**SLIME THICKNESS**

up to ¹⁴/₁,₀₀₀ mm (on fish found with anemones)

up to ⁵/₁,₀₀₀ mm (on fish not found with anemones)

Clownfish skin is slimier than the skin of other fish—which may stop the anemone from firing its stings.

**DISTANCE TRAVELED**

| ft | 4 | 8 | 12 |
| m | 2 | | 4 |

9¾ ft/3 m (max. from sea anemone)

**TIME SPENT AS LARVAE**

8–12 DAYS

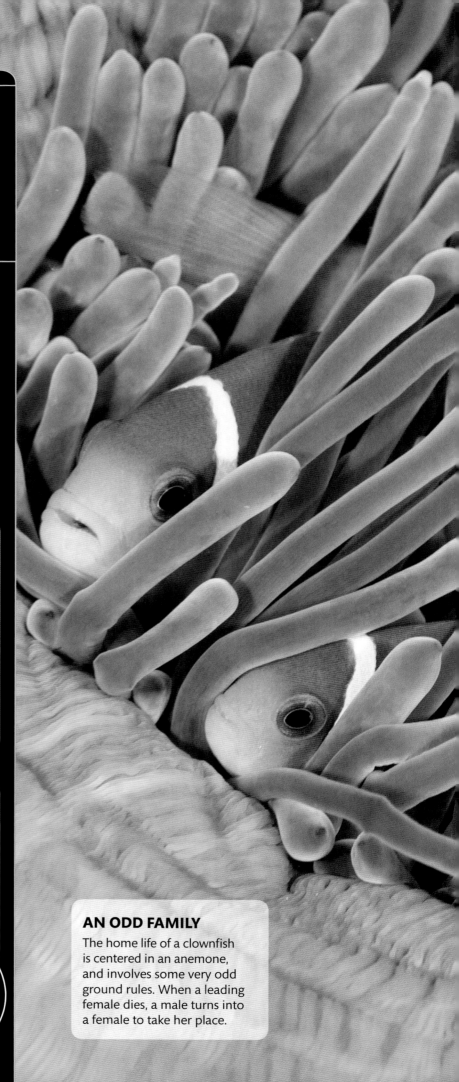

### AN ODD FAMILY

The home life of a clownfish is centered in an anemone, and involves some very odd ground rules. When a leading female dies, a male turns into a female to take her place.

# UPSTREAM MARAUDER
## BULL SHARK

**Almost all sharks need salty ocean water** to survive, but the bull shark is just as happy in fresh water. Bull sharks regularly swim up rivers, sometimes for thousands of miles. In some parts of the world they even cross rocky rapids in their river journeys. Coming so far inland can bring them close to popular bathing spots, where they have been known to attack humans.

## AT A GLANCE

- **SIZE** 7½–11½ ft (2.3–3.5 m) long
- **HABITAT** Warm and tropical coastal ocean waters, and large river systems
- **LOCATION** Near coastlines in tropical regions
- **DIET** Fish, including other sharks, turtles, birds, dolphins, and some land-living mammals

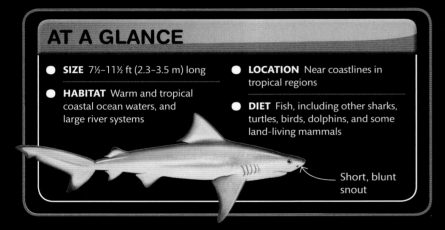

Short, blunt snout

## STATS AND FACTS

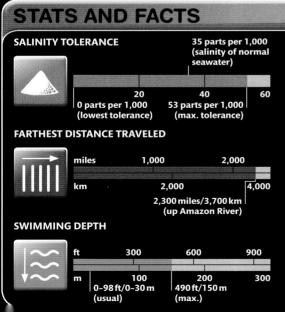

**SALINITY TOLERANCE**

35 parts per 1,000 (salinity of normal seawater)

| | 20 | 40 | 60 |
|---|---|---|---|
0 parts per 1,000 (lowest tolerance) | | 53 parts per 1,000 (max. tolerance) | |

**FARTHEST DISTANCE TRAVELED**

| miles | 1,000 | 2,000 | |
|---|---|---|---|
| km | 2,000 | | 4,000 |

2,300 miles/3,700 km (up Amazon River)

**SWIMMING DEPTH**

| ft | 300 | 600 | 900 |
|---|---|---|---|
| m | 100 | 200 | 300 |

0–98 ft/0–30 m (usual)    490 ft/150 m (max.)

Many sharks enter river estuaries, but only bull sharks routinely go inland. Farther upstream, the salinity, or saltiness, of the ocean drops as salty water is replaced by fresh water. Most sharks die without salt in the water, but the bull shark does just as well in rivers as in the ocean.

## BEACH CRUISER

There is plenty of prey close to shorelines, and even more in estuaries and rivers. Bull sharks catch fish wherever they go, but big ones may even attack land animals that venture into the water.

# ANGLING FOR TROUBLE

Bull sharks are perfectly at home in the cloudy waters of river estuaries. Tides, waves, and bad weather stir up the mud at the mouths of rivers. Despite this, bull sharks can still sense their prey through the murky water. They are drawn to activity along the river, often inspecting fishing boats or even anglers on the shore. By cruising into the shallows they hope to make a grab for anything that ventures into the water.

"A bull shark **head-butts** its prey to disorient it before taking **a bite**"

# UNDERWATER VALET

## BLUE-STREAK CLEANER WRASSE

**It can be difficult for a fish to stay clean** and healthy on a busy ocean reef. The reef has tiny animals called parasites that cling to fish to eat their skin and blood. The blue-streak cleaner wrasse is nature's answer to this problem. It patrols a spot on the reef that other fish know well. When one of them visits, the wrasse greets its "customer" with a little dance, before nibbling away to remove its parasites and giving the fish a thorough grooming.

### AT A GLANCE

- **SIZE** 5½–8½ in (14–22 cm) long

- **HABITAT** Coral reefs and lagoons, staying close to "cleaning stations"

- **LOCATION** Red Sea and near coastlines of Indian Ocean and western Pacific Ocean

- **DIET** Parasites and slime from the bodies of other fish

### STATS AND FACTS

**4 YEARS MAXIMUM LIFESPAN**

**NUMBER OF PARASITES EATEN PER DAY**

| | 500 | 1,000 | 1,500 |
|---|---|---|---|

1,100–1,340

**CUSTOMERS AT CLEANING STATION**

| | 20 | 30 | 40 | 50 |
|---|---|---|---|---|

20–50 species of fish per day

**CUSTOMERS PER DAY**

**100**

## CLEANING THE GILLS

The tiny cleaner wrasse gets food by eating parasites. Its client stays still while the wrasse sets to work over its body, sometimes going right inside the gills for a really deep clean.

# TIDEPOOL CRAWLER

## BROWN-BANDED BAMBOO SHARK

**Being a small shark has its advantages.** The slim-bodied bamboo shark has no trouble living in shallow pools around tropical coastlines, where it can get plenty of food by reaching between rocks for prey. It is so at home that it is not even bothered by the tides. Other fish must scurry into deeper water when the tide goes out, but the bamboo shark is happy to find a moist spot and wait for the water to return.

### AT A GLANCE

- **SIZE** 3–4 ft (0.9-1.2 m) long

- **HABITAT** Coral reefs and tidal pools

- **LOCATION** Coastlines of northern Indian Ocean and western Pacific, including India, Philippines, Japan, and Australia

- **DIET** Small bottom-living fish, worms, and crabs

Bands hardly visible on adult shark

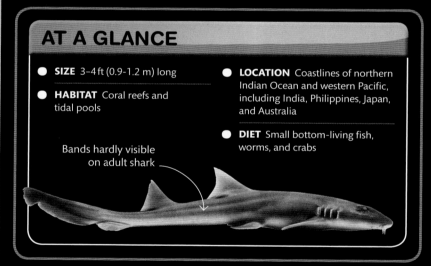

### STATS AND FACTS

**WALKING SPEED**

| | mph | 0.3 | 0.6 |
|---|---|---|---|
| | km/h | 0.5 | 1 |

0.4 mph
(0.6 km/h) est.

In shallow pools, bamboo sharks can use their strong pectoral fins for "walking" over rocks, sometimes emerging from the water.

**DEPTH**

| | ft | 100 | 200 | 300 |
|---|---|---|---|---|
| | m | 25 | 50 | 75 | 100 |

0-278 ft (0-85 m)

MAX. TIME OUT OF WATER
**12**
HOURS

## BANDED BABY

Most sharks lack distinct markings, but young bamboo sharks have bold dark bands around their body. As the babies grow to adult size these bands fade until only the plain color remains.

**109**

# STUPENDOUS SWARM
## ANTARCTIC KRILL

**Try to imagine a crowd of animals** with a thousand times more individuals than there are people in the whole world. Shrimplike krill swim in the open ocean and get together in colossal swarms that are the biggest on the planet. Each krill catches tiny morsels of food with its feathery legs. The huge weight of a tightly packed swarm of krill is, in turn, food for many bigger animals including fish, whales, seals, and penguins.

## AT A GLANCE

- **SIZE** Up to 2½ in (6.5 cm) long
- **HABITAT** Cold open ocean
- **LOCATION** Southern Ocean; most abundant around the Antarctic continent and islands
- **DIET** Green plankton, such as microscopic algae

## STATS AND FACTS

**KRILL IN A SWARM**

30,000 per 35 cu ft
(30,000 per cu m)

| 0 | 15,000 | 30,000 | 45,000 |

The biggest and densest swarms of krill are made up of younger, more buoyant individuals. Mature krill need more room and live in scattered swarms that are one-tenth as large.

**TOTAL WEIGHT**

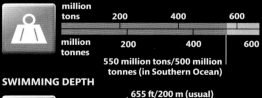

| million tons | 200 | 400 | 600 |
| million tonnes | 200 | 400 | 600 |

550 million tons/500 million tonnes (in Southern Ocean)

**SWIMMING DEPTH**

655 ft/200 m (usual)

| ft | 500 | 1,000 | 1,500 |
| m | | 300 | 600 |

1,575 ft/480 m (max.)

EGGS LAID AT A TIME

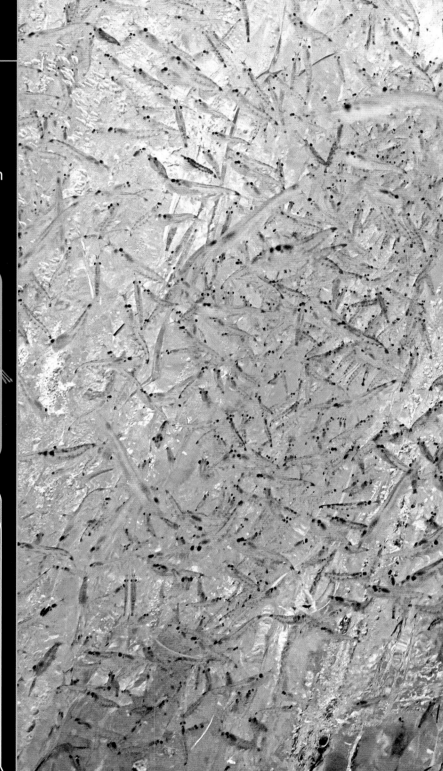

"Krill can **flash** like little **headlights** to confuse predators"

**FEEDING SWARM**

Every day billions of krill move up from the depths to feed on algae growing on the underside of the ice sheets. The huge swarms cause a feeding frenzy among fish and birds waiting near the surface.

111

"The big **blunt head** of the megamouth has led to it being **mistaken for an orca**"

# MYSTERIOUS GIANT
## MEGAMOUTH SHARK

**The ocean is big enough** to hide its secrets for a long time, even something as big as the megamouth shark. This deep-sea giant wasn't discovered until 1976, when one was caught off Hawaii, and hasn't been seen much since. It feeds on swimming shrimplike animals called krill by gulping in seawater and filtering out the tiny prey using its gills.

## AT A GLANCE

- **SIZE** 13–18 ft (4–5.5 m) long

- **HABITAT** Mainly open ocean in warm regions, but also seen near the shore

- **LOCATION** Widespread in the subtropics and tropics; recorded from California, Brazil, Africa, Japan, SE Asia, Australia, and Hawaii

- **DIET** Mainly krill and small shrimp, but also some jellyfish

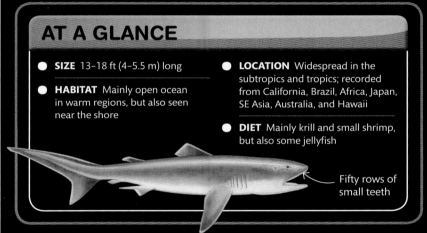

Fifty rows of small teeth

## STATS AND FACTS

The megamouth has fewer prey-detecting sensory pores on its short snout than longer-nosed sharks, but they are still effective for detecting food. It tracks krill at the surface by day and to deeper water at night.

**DEPTH DURING THE NIGHT**

0–655 ft/0–200 m (depth of krill)

| ft | 300 | 600 |

| m | 100 | 200 |

395–545 ft/120–165 m (feeding depth)

**DEPTH DURING THE DAY**

0–130 ft/0–40 m (depth of krill)

| ft | 300 | 600 |

| m | 100 | 200 |

40–82 ft/12–25 m (feeding depth)

**NO. OF SENSORY PORES**

225 (total)

48 (on side of head)

169 (on top of head)    8 (beneath head)

**NO. OF SIGHTINGS**

**63**

### SECRET SUCKER

Although no one has seen a megamouth feeding, scientists think that it sticks out its huge jaws to suck in water. Tiny swimming animals, such as krill, are then trapped by bristlelike rakers on the gills.

# INSIDE-OUT TRICKSTER
## SEA CUCUMBER

An animal that looks like a juicy sausage is sure to attract the attentions of a predator, but a sea cucumber may not be such a tasty feast. This flabby-bodied, slow-moving animal lives on the sea floor and seems quite helpless. Some types of sea cucumbers have bright colors as a warning that they contain poisons in their flesh. If that doesn't work, they resort to drastic measures: they squirt out their innards in a sticky mess—usually enough to send the hungriest prowler on its way.

Water pressure inflates tube feet

### TUBE FEET

A sea cucumber has suckerlike tube feet that each extend by the pressure of water inside them until the sucker sticks to a surface. When the pressure drops, the foot lifts. Together the tube feet haul the animal forwards.

### AT A GLANCE

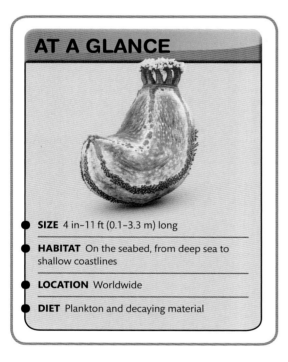

- **SIZE** 4 in–11 ft (0.1–3.3 m) long
- **HABITAT** On the seabed, from deep sea to shallow coastlines
- **LOCATION** Worldwide
- **DIET** Plankton and decaying material

"Sea cucumbers **regrow** their body **organs** in **two weeks**"

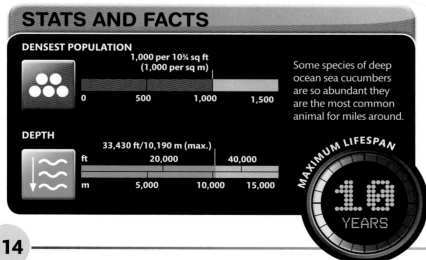

Five rows of tube feet along the body for moving slowly over surfaces

Bright orange and red markings as warning

### STATS AND FACTS

**DENSEST POPULATION**

1,000 per 10¾ sq ft (1,000 per sq m)

| 0 | 500 | 1,000 | 1,500 |
|---|-----|-------|-------|

Some species of deep ocean sea cucumbers are so abundant they are the most common animal for miles around.

**DEPTH**

33,430 ft/10,190 m (max.)

| ft | 20,000 | 40,000 |
|----|--------|--------|
| m | 5,000 | 10,000 | 15,000 |

MAXIMUM LIFESPAN

**10 YEARS**

Bristly tips of feeding tentacles move around to trap food particles in surrounding seawater

## TENTACLE EXTENSION

The bristly tentacles around the mouth of a sea cucumber are extra-long tube feet (see left). They are used like sticky fingers to trap any food particles floating by and feed them into the body.

Sea apple swallows water to swell up when alarmed

**Colorful oddity**

The sea apple is an especially brightly colored species of sea cucumber but it is not as delicious as its fruity name suggests—it releases a foul soapy substance when alarmed.

## INNARDS OUT

It is difficult to tell if a sea cucumber is startled until it suddenly does its nasty inside-out trick. This is a sea cucumber's secret weapon to defend itself. By using muscles to squeeze its body wall, the sea cucumber's gut shoots straight out of its bottom. Sometimes this is mixed with special tacky threads too—as seen here—and they will stick to the face of any predatory fish that comes too close. Amazingly, sea cucumbers have no trouble completely rebuilding their insides after this has happened.

# CRAB KILLER
## STARRY SMOOTH-HOUND

**Strong jaws are more important** than cutting teeth when you spend your life munching on crabs. The starry smooth-hound, named for the small, white, star-shaped markings on its body, eats little else and has done away with biting blades altogether. Instead, its mouth has rows of tiny overlapping teeth that act as a rough grinding surface, perfect for taking a firm hold on a crab's shell. Then it is up to the powerful jaw muscles to crunch through to the meat.

### AT A GLANCE

- **SIZE** 4½–5 ft (1.4–1.5 m)
- **HABITAT** Coastal marine waters with sandy and gravelly bottoms
- **LOCATION** Northeastern Atlantic Ocean, North Sea, and Mediterranean Sea
- **DIET** Mainly crabs, hermit crabs, and lobsters

### STATS AND FACTS

**MAXIMUM DEPTH**

| ft | 300 | 600 | 900 | 1,200 |
|---|---|---|---|---|
| m | 100 | 200 | 300 | 400 |

1,150 ft (350 m)

The starry smooth-hound swims close to the bottom, where it is most likely to find its favorite prey: crabs and lobsters.

**DIET**

56% swimming crabs

34% other crustaceans

2% fish

7% hermit crabs

1% sea cucumbers

**Starry shark**
The tiny white stars that pepper the back of a starry smooth-hound are clear in some individuals, but indistinct or even missing in others.

> "Smooth-hounds feed in groups – just like a **pack** of dogs!"

Second dorsal fin slightly smaller than first dorsal fin

Long tail with notch

Broad, round mouth contains rows of small crushing teeth

# LONG-LIVED HUNTER
## SPINY DOGFISH

**The spiny dogfish** might be one of the smallest sharks in the ocean, but what it lacks in size it makes up for in ferocity. It hunts in packs and does not hesitate to attack big prey. Its jaws and teeth work like shears to cut flesh. Although it is an active predator, it lives its life at a slow pace, and lives longer than many larger sharks.

**"Spiny dogfish often bite through nets to eat a fisherman's catch"**

Large eyes help it hunt in deep, dark water

White venomous spine on front of each dorsal fin

White spots along the back

### Sting in the fin
The spiny dogfish gets its name from the short spines in front of its dorsal fins. They are mildly venomous, but the dogfish has to arch its back to stab attackers.

## AT A GLANCE

Body is paler below than on the back

- **SIZE** 2¼–5¼ ft (0.7–1.6 m) long
- **HABITAT** Deep ocean waters near the coast
- **LOCATION** North Atlantic, North Pacific, and close to southern coastlines of South America, South Africa, Australia, and New Zealand
- **DIET** Fish, squid, octopuses, crabs, and jellyfish

## STATS AND FACTS

**AGE TO BECOME MATURE**

6 years (for males)

12 years (for females)

**SIZE**

27–63 in/69–160 cm (full size)

| in | 15 | 30 | 45 | 60 |
|----|----|----|----|----|
| cm | 40 | 80 | 120 | 160 |

8–12 in/20–30 cm (at birth)

**75 YEARS** MAXIMUM RECORDED AGE

**22 MONTHS** MAX. GESTATION PERIOD

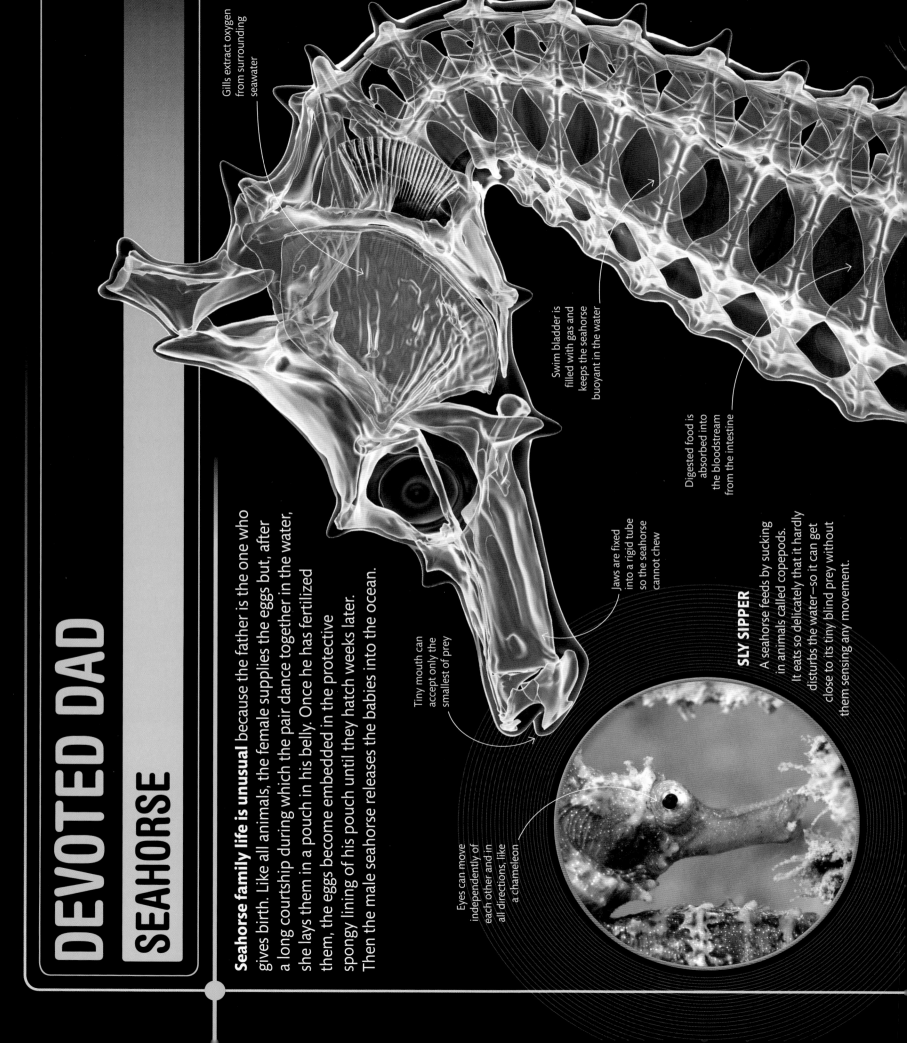

# DEVOTED DAD
## SEAHORSE

**Seahorse family life is unusual** because the father is the one who gives birth. Like all animals, the female supplies the eggs but, after a long courtship during which the pair dance together in the water, she lays them in a pouch in his belly. Once he has fertilized them, the eggs become embedded in the protective spongy lining of his pouch until they hatch weeks later. Then the male seahorse releases the babies into the ocean.

Gills extract oxygen from surrounding seawater

Swim bladder is filled with gas and keeps the seahorse buoyant in the water

Digested food is absorbed into the bloodstream from the intestine

Jaws are fixed into a rigid tube so the seahorse cannot chew

Tiny mouth can accept only the smallest of prey

### SLY SIPPER

A seahorse feeds by sucking in animals called copepods. It eats so delicately that it hardly disturbs the water—so it can get close to its tiny blind prey without them sensing any movement.

Eyes can move independently of each other and in all directions, like a chameleon

Dorsal fin flutters to propel the seahorse forward

Scaleless skin covers bony plates

Male's pouch swells up when it is filled with eggs

## A LONG BIRTH

Seahorse babies get food and oxygen in their dad's pouch—just like in a real pregnancy. When the time comes he may even suffer hours of contractions to release them into the water.

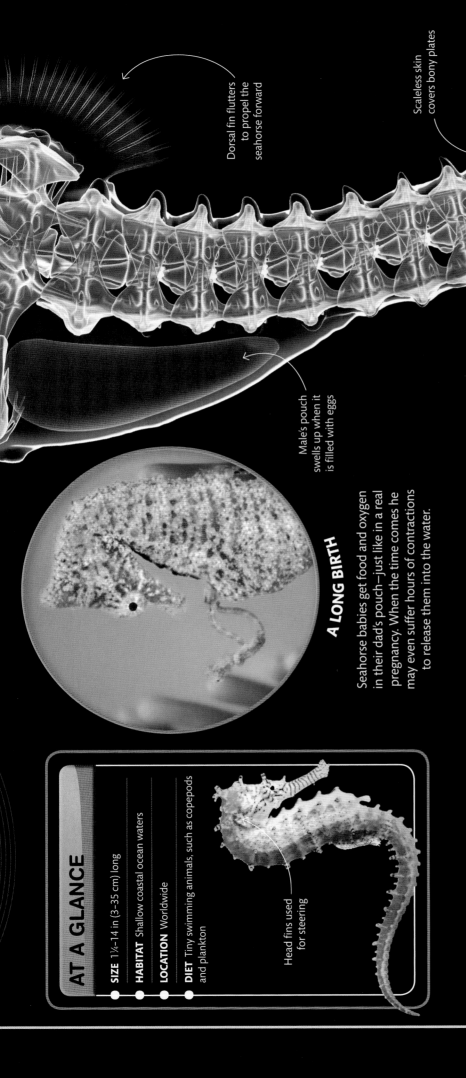

## Armor plating

Seahorses are named for their upright posture and the shape of their head. They are very slow swimmers, but their entire body is encased in a casing of bony plates, which gives some protection from predators.

Long tail is prehensile, meaning it can be used to grip objects

## AT A GLANCE

**SIZE** 1¼–14 in (3–35 cm) long

**HABITAT** Shallow coastal ocean waters

**LOCATION** Worldwide

**DIET** Tiny swimming animals, such as copepods and plankton

Head fins used for steering

## STATS AND FACTS

There are more than 50 species of seahorses. The largest ones usually live longer, have longer pregnancies, and produce more babies per brood.

**LENGTH**

| in | ¼ | ½ | ¾ | 1 | 2 | 3 |
|----|----|----|----|----|----|----|
| cm | 1 | | | 1/16–12/16 in/0.2–2 cm (young at birth) | | |

**DURATION OF PREGNANCY**

| days | 10 | 20 | 30 | 40 | 50 |
|------|----|----|----|----|----|
| | | | 9–45 days | | |

**AGE**

| months | 3 | 6 | 9 | 12 | 15 |
|--------|---|---|---|----|----|
| | | 3–12 months (age breeding starts) | | | |

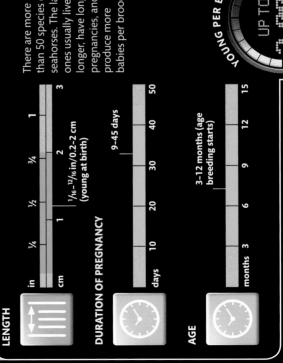

YOUNG PER BROOD

UP TO 2,000

**SPOTTED SUCKER**
Zebra sharks spend their time cruising slowly around coral reefs. They catch their prey by sucking animals that live on the ocean floor out of the sand and into their mouth.

# COSTUME CHANGER
## ZEBRA SHARK

**The first scientists to describe this shark** had only a zebra-striped youngster to go on, which is how the species got its name. As the shark grows bigger, it changes its skin pattern and the stripes are replaced with leopardlike spots. Newborn zebra sharks are especially striking, with a distinct black body and thin white bands. It is possible that this protects them from danger because predators think they are banded sea snakes, which are highly venomous. If true, this may be the only case where a shark mimics the appearance of another kind of animal.

## AT A GLANCE

- **SIZE** 4¾–7¾ ft (1.45–2.35 m) long

- **HABITAT** Shallow tropical waters near the ocean floor—especially on coral reefs and sandy banks; sometimes enters brackish waters

- **LOCATION** Red Sea and coastal areas of the Indian and western Pacific Oceans

- **DIET** Snails, small fish, crabs, shrimp, and sea snakes

## STATS AND FACTS

Baby zebra sharks must grow to more than twice their hatching size before their stripes start changing to spots.

MAXIMUM LIFESPAN

**30** YEARS

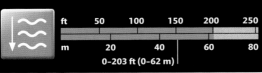
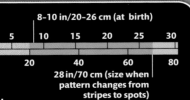

# DEMON STINGER
## SPINY DEVILFISH

**The spiny devilfish** is almost impossible to spot on a brightly colored bed of a tropical reef. Sometimes it is even half buried in the sand. The devilfish crawls along the ocean floor using its fins like legs. Then it waits very still for prey to come close before lunging with its enormous mouth. It has little to fear: with venomous spines sticking up from its back, it will give a nasty shock to any shark unwise enough to make a grab. These dangerous spines have even been known to kill a human.

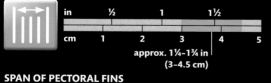

## AT A GLANCE

- **SIZE** 7–10 in (18–25 cm)
- **HABITAT** Coral reefs, lagoons, and sometimes around estuaries—usually over sand or mud, and often buried so it cannot be seen
- **LOCATION** Eastern Indian Ocean and western Pacific from China south to Australia
- **DIET** Small fish, shrimp, and crabs

## STATS AND FACTS

**SPINE LENGTH**

| in | ½ | 1 | 1½ |
|----|----|----|----|
| cm | 1 | 2 | 3 | 4 | 5 |

approx. 1¼–1¾ in (3–4.5 cm)

The venomous spines of the devilfish form part of the fin that runs along its back. They stick up when danger threatens.

**SPAN OF PECTORAL FINS**

| in | 2 | 4 | 6 | 8 |
|----|----|----|----|----|
| cm | 5 | 10 | 15 | 20 | 25 |

approx. 6–9 in (15–22 cm)

VENOMOUS SPINES

UP TO

## STINGING AMBUSH

The devilfish's skin is covered in wrinkles and warts to help it blend in with the surrounding coral and seaweed. It is a slow swimmer and cannot catch a meal simply by chasing it, so it needs to take prey by surprise.

"The frilled shark's ancestry dates back to **150 million** years ago"

# LIVING FOSSIL
## FRILLED SHARK

**Looking more like a mythical sea snake** than a shark, this deep-sea monster belongs to a group of sharks whose beginnings stretch far back to the time of the dinosaurs. The frilled shark is strange in many ways. Its spine is incomplete, so its back is supported by a rubbery rod, and it has six gill slits, whereas most sharks have five. Its head looks as though it should belong to a lizard, and inside its wide jaws there are hundreds of three-pronged needle-sharp teeth that can bite slippery squid.

### AT A GLANCE

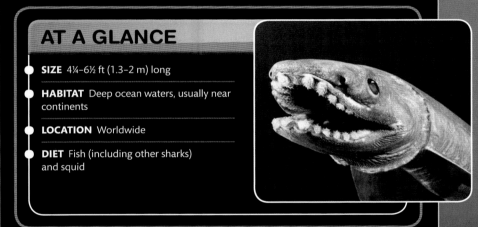

- **SIZE** 4¼–6½ ft (1.3–2 m) long
- **HABITAT** Deep ocean waters, usually near continents
- **LOCATION** Worldwide
- **DIET** Fish (including other sharks) and squid

### STATS AND FACTS

Like most other kinds of sharks, frilled sharks give birth to live young. However, their pregnancy is one of the longest of any kind of animal.

**SWIMMING DEPTH**

| ft | | 2,000 | | 4,000 |
| m | 500 | 1,000 | | 1,500 |

395–4,200 ft
(120–1,280 m)

**PUPS PER LITTER**

| 0 | 5 | 10 | 15 |

2–12

**SIZE OF PUPS AT BIRTH**

| in | 15 | 30 |
| cm | 20 | 40 | 60 | 80 |

16–23½ in (40–60 cm)

**GESTATION PERIOD**

### FRILLY FACE

The frilled shark gets its name from the ruffled gill edges that connect underneath its head to form a collar. This strange shark

# MOST DEVOTED MOTHER

## COMMON OCTOPUS

**It's a short life for an octopus**—sometimes not much more than a year—but up to two months of that can be taken up with raising a huge family. An octopus mother produces around a quarter of a million eggs, which she hangs in strings from rocks. She gives up hunting to concentrate on looking after her brood and protecting them from predators. By the time they hatch she is usually so weak from starvation that she dies.

Mantle, or fleshy cloak, contains vital organs

Well-developed eyes for good underwater vision

### Getting around

An octopus uses eight muscular arms for walking on the bottom of the sea. But for a really fast getaway it uses jet propulsion by shooting a jet of water from a fleshy funnel.

### BITING BEAK

The beak is the only hard part of an octopus's body. It lies in the center of the body and is strong enough to crunch up most prey, including tough-shelled crabs and lobsters.

Head contains big brain

### AT A GLANCE

- **SIZE** 5–9¾ ft (1.5–3 m) tentacle span
- **HABITAT** Rocky coastal waters
- **LOCATION** Atlantic, Indian, and west Pacific Oceans; Mediterranean Sea
- **DIET** Crabs, crayfish, cockles, and other shelled animals

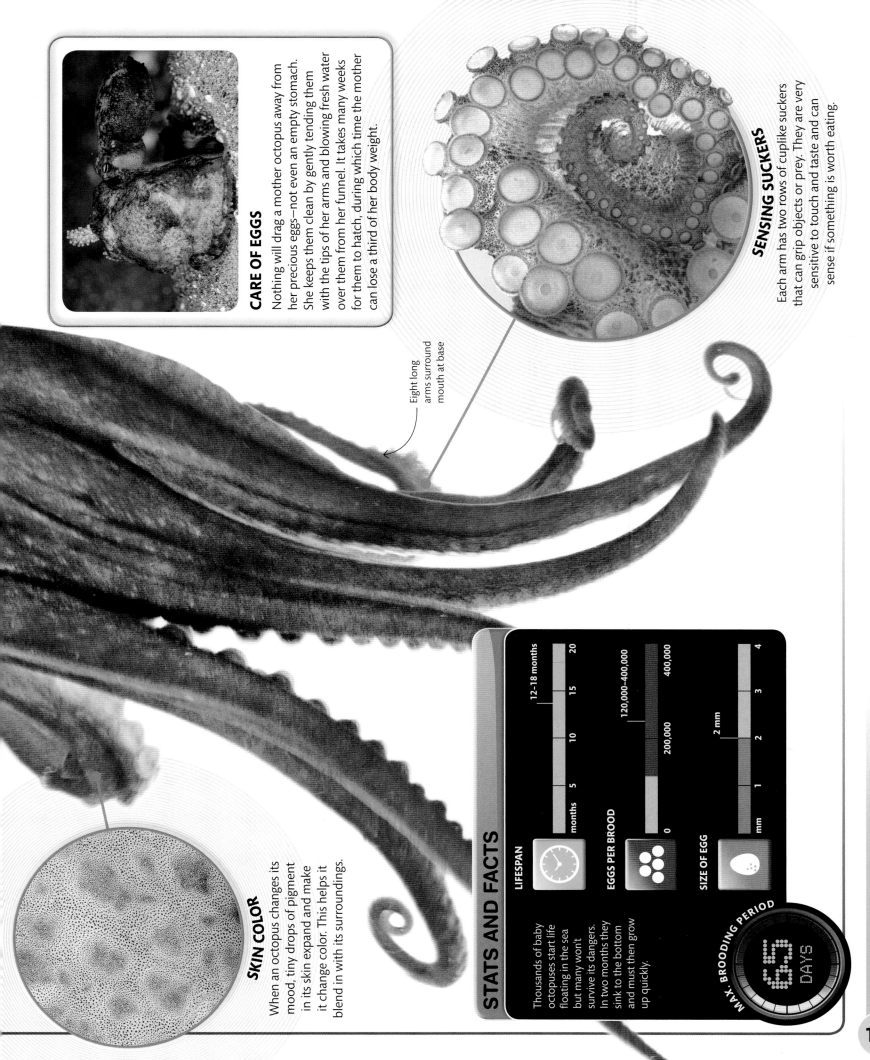

## CARE OF EGGS

Nothing will drag a mother octopus away from her precious eggs—not even an empty stomach. She keeps them clean by gently tending them with the tips of her arms and blowing fresh water over them from her funnel. It takes many weeks for them to hatch, during which time the mother can lose a third of her body weight.

## SENSING SUCKERS

Each arm has two rows of cuplike suckers that can grip objects or prey. They are very sensitive to touch and taste and can sense if something is worth eating.

Eight long arms surround mouth at base

## SKIN COLOR

When an octopus changes its mood, tiny drops of pigment in its skin expand and make it change color. This helps it blend in with its surroundings.

## STATS AND FACTS

| LIFESPAN | months | 5 | 10 | 15 | 12–18 months | 20 |
|---|---|---|---|---|---|---|
| EGGS PER BROOD | 0 | 200,000 | 120,000–400,000 | 400,000 | |
| SIZE OF EGG | mm | 1 | 2 mm | 2 | 3 | 4 |

Thousands of baby octopuses start life floating in the sea but many won't survive its dangers. In two months they sink to the bottom and must then grow up quickly.

MAX. BROODING PERIOD

42 DAYS

# STRANDING SURVIVOR
## BLIND SHARK

**This shark shuns the open ocean** and instead spends its life right beside the warm Australian coastline. It is rarely seen during the day because it hides in caves and under rocky ledges. At night it emerges to hunt for small animals on the coral reef. Despite its name, it has reasonably good vision, but if it finds itself exposed to danger, it can pull its vulnerable eyeballs inward and close them with thick eyelids. It can also survive for many hours out of water if it is stranded among rocks when the tide is low.

### AT A GLANCE

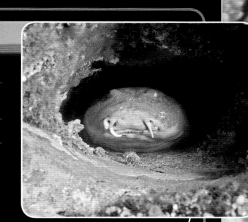

- **SIZE** 3¼–4 ft (1–1.2 m) long
- **HABITAT** Rocky shorelines, coral reefs, and beds of seagrass
- **LOCATION** Eastern coast of Australia
- **DIET** Small fish, cuttlefish, crabs, and sea anemones

### STATS AND FACTS

By squinting when out of water, the blind shark can prevent its eyeballs from drying out, and protect them from danger.

**EYE SIZE**

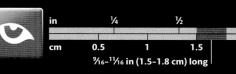

| in | | ¼ | ½ | ¾ |
|---|---|---|---|---|
| cm | 0.5 | 1 | 1.5 | 2 |

⁹⁄₁₆–¹¹⁄₁₆ in (1.5–1.8 cm) long

**DEPTH**

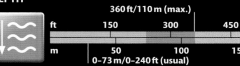

360 ft/110 m (max.)

| ft | 150 | 300 | 450 |
|---|---|---|---|
| m | 50 | 100 | 150 |

0–73 m/0–240 ft (usual)

**MAX. TIME OUT OF WATER**

### SENSING PREY

Although it has normal vision, the blind shark also uses sensory feelers on the front of its head to sense small animal prey among tangles

# BURROW BOLTER
## GARDEN EEL

**In the shallows of the ocean** a colony of eels pokes out from a patch of sand, looking more like a sprouting reedy garden than a group of fish. They snap at tiny animals floating by in the water, but keep a firm hold on their burrows. If any danger threatens they can dart straight back into the sand, tail first. A long body allows garden eels to get almost everything they need within reach of their burrows, so they rarely venture out for a swim.

## AT A GLANCE

- **SIZE** 12–47 in (30–121 cm) long
- **HABITAT** Marine coastal waters, in colonies in coral sand
- **LOCATION** Worldwide, but with greatest number of species in eastern Indian Ocean and western Pacific Ocean
- **DIET** Small planktonic animals

## STATS AND FACTS

Garden eels stretch out of their burrows leaving a quarter of their body length inside. Neighboring burrows are far enough away to avoid squabbles over food.

**DISTANCE BETWEEN NEIGHBORS**

| in | | 5 | | 10 | |
|----|----|----|----|----|----|
| cm | 10 | | 20 | | 30 |

9¾ in (25 cm) minimum

**DISTANCE EEL EMERGES**

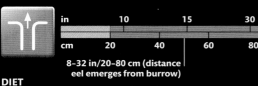

| in | | 10 | 15 | | 30 |
|----|----|----|----|----|----|
| cm | 20 | 40 | | 60 | 80 |

8–32 in/20–80 cm (distance eel emerges from burrow)

**DIET**

19% tiny soft-bodied animals

66% tiny shrimplike animals

15% eggs and larvae

**BIGGEST COLONY**

1,000

## ON THE LOOKOUT

Dozens of garden eels face into a stream of plankton carried on the ocean current. If a pair of eyes spots danger, an eel retreats into the burrow, and all the others do the same.

**REEF ROVER**

Named for the markings on its dorsal fins and tail, the whitetip reef shark is one of the main predators of tropical reefs, but it is often docile toward humans.

# CAVE CRUISER

## WHITETIP REEF SHARK

**There are plenty of places to hide** on a rocky coral reef, but some hungry sharks will do their best to search all the crevices. The whitetip reef shark has especially tough skin and a slender body for reaching deep between rocks. Ridges over its eyes, giving it a permanently angry look, provide extra protection. This fish prowls around at night, exploring caves in search of prey, specializing in hunting animals that live on the bottom.

### AT A GLANCE

- **SIZE** 5¼–6½ ft (1.6–2 m)

- **HABITAT** Clear coastal waters around coral reefs, often resting in caves

- **LOCATION** Widespread in the tropics and subtropics

- **DIET** Bottom-living animals, including fish, octopuses, crabs, and lobsters

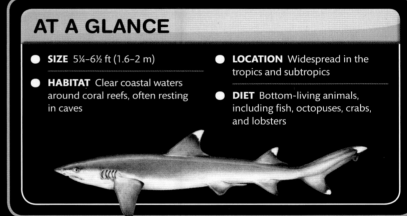

### STATS AND FACTS

**CRUISING DEPTH**

26–130 ft/8–40 m (usual)

| ft | 300 | 600 | 900 | 1,200 |
| m | 100 | 200 | 300 | 400 |

1,080 ft/330 m
(max. depth recorded)

**TIME SPENT SWIMMING**

1–3 hrs (during the day)

5–8 hrs (at night)

**DISTANCE TRAVELED FROM HOME**

| miles | ½ | 1 | 1½ | 2 |
| km | 1 | 2 | 3 | 4 |

0.25–1.8 miles (0.3–3 km) in 1 year

The whitetip reef shark has a very small home range and rarely travels far from its favorite hunting spots. It sleeps during the day in underwater caves.

# SHELLFISH SMASHER
## SEA OTTER

**It can be tricky to break the hard shell** of a mussel or a crab. For a hungry sea otter, a small rock is the perfect tool for smashing through to reach the meat. When it finds a shellfish, a sea otter lies on its back with its dinner on its belly. Then, grasping the rock in its front paws, it bangs hard until the shell cracks. This works so well that some otters even carry a rock around with them under a special flap of skin in their armpit. A life spent fishing for seafood is a cold one and the sea otter keeps warm with a thick coat—the densest coat of any mammal.

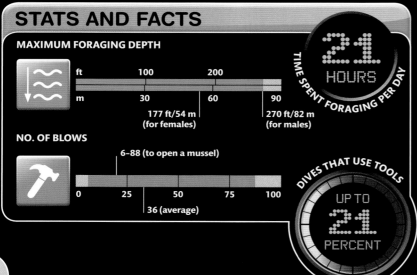

## AT A GLANCE

- **SIZE** Head and body 3¼–4 ft (1–1.2 m) long; tail 10–14½ in (25–37 cm) long
- **HABITAT** Shoreline and shallow ocean waters within 0.6 miles (1 km) of coast
- **LOCATION** Northeastern Russia and western coastal North America
- **DIET** Slow-swimming fish, sea urchins, crabs, and mollusks

## STATS AND FACTS

**MAXIMUM FORAGING DEPTH**

| ft | 100 | 200 | |
|---|---|---|---|
| m | 30 | 60 | 90 |

177 ft/54 m (for females)
270 ft/82 m (for males)

**NO. OF BLOWS**

6–88 (to open a mussel)

| 0 | 25 | 50 | 75 | 100 |
|---|---|---|---|---|

36 (average)

**21 HOURS** TIME SPENT FORAGING PER DAY

**UP TO 21 PERCENT** DIVES THAT USE TOOLS

"Some sea otters even have a favorite rock"

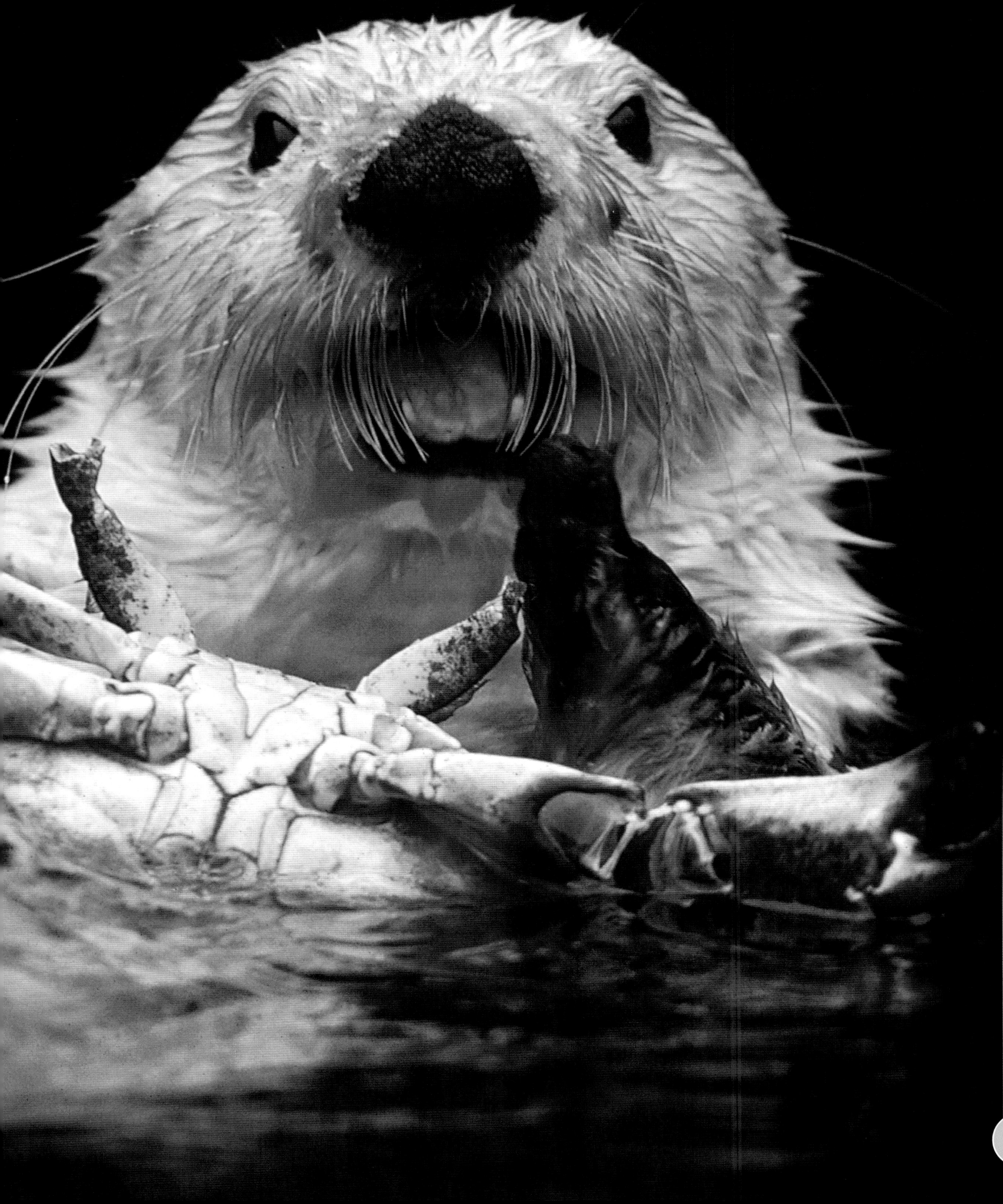

# WOLF OF THE SEA
## BLUE SHARK

**When sharks come together** and work as a pack they can make a terrifying hunting team. Blue sharks live in the open ocean. To catch their favorite prey—schools of fish and squid—they use the same tactics as a wolf. Groups of blue sharks swim around a school so that the prey bunch closer together. They then sweep in to grab a mouthful. Blue sharks prefer lower temperatures than other reef sharks, but are found in oceans around the world. When they reach the tropics, they swim deeper to stay in cooler water.

## AT A GLANCE

- **SIZE** 7¼–12 ft (2.2–3.8 m) long
- **HABITAT** Mainly in the open ocean, but occasionally coming near to coastlines; younger sharks live in more coastal waters
- **LOCATION** Worldwide except in the coldest polar waters; one of the most widespread of all sharks
- **DIET** Mainly fish and squid of the open ocean

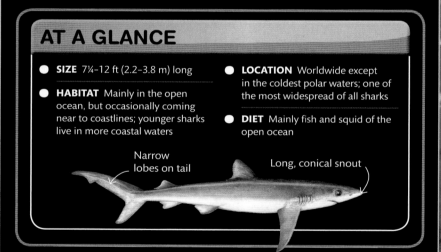

Narrow lobes on tail

Long, conical snout

## STATS AND FACTS

**SWIMMING SPEED**

25 mph (40 km/h)

| mph | 10 | 20 | 30 | |
| km/h | 20 | 40 | 60 |

Blue sharks give birth to live young and have some of the biggest litters among sharks.

**GESTATION PERIOD**

9–12

| months | 5 | 10 | 15 |

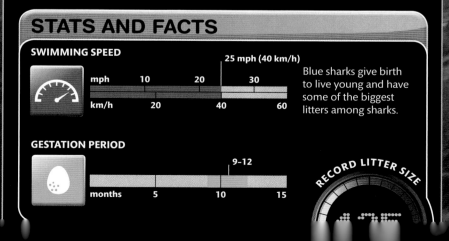

RECORD LITTER SIZE

## BLUE IN THE SEA

The blue color of this shark is a perfect disguise as it circles a school of krill. Like many sharks, it has a white underside, a feature that hides it from

"The blue shark is highly **migratory,** traveling distances of up to **5,720 miles** (9,200 km)"

# SUPER CLUTCH
## LOGGERHEAD TURTLE

**Turtles live in fresh and salty waters**—but marine turtles grow much bigger than their cousins on land. Instead of legs they have huge, paddlelike flippers that are ideal for swimming, so they spend most of their lives in the ocean. All turtles produce shelled eggs, so even ocean species have to visit the shore to lay them—producing more than a hundred at a time.

Baby turtles hatch from round, leathery eggs

Upper shell is slightly heart-shaped and made up of horny plates

Ovaries can produce as many as 200 eggs at a time

### RACE TO THE SEA

Loggerhead turtles bury their eggs on sandy beaches, well out of reach of the tide. When they hatch, the babies have to dig their way out—before waddling as fast as they can to the ocean.

Two or three claws on each back flipper

Lower shell (plastron) is flatter and has fewer plates

Back flippers are used for swimming and digging nests

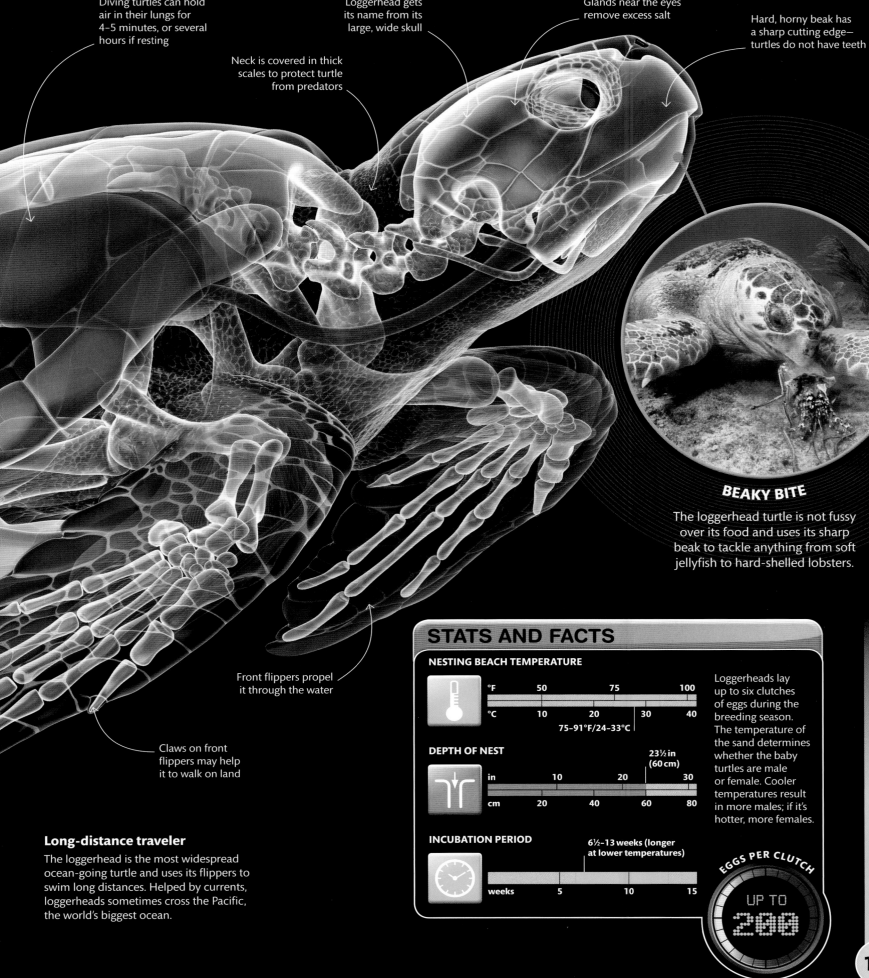

Diving turtles can hold air in their lungs for 4–5 minutes, or several hours if resting

Loggerhead gets its name from its large, wide skull

Glands near the eyes remove excess salt

Hard, horny beak has a sharp cutting edge— turtles do not have teeth

Neck is covered in thick scales to protect turtle from predators

Front flippers propel it through the water

Claws on front flippers may help it to walk on land

## BEAKY BITE

The loggerhead turtle is not fussy over its food and uses its sharp beak to tackle anything from soft jellyfish to hard-shelled lobsters.

## STATS AND FACTS

**NESTING BEACH TEMPERATURE**

| °F | 50 | 75 | 100 |
| °C | 10 | 20 | 30 | 40 |

75–91°F/24–33°C

**DEPTH OF NEST**

23½ in (60 cm)

| in | 10 | 20 | 30 |
| cm | 20 | 40 | 60 | 80 |

**INCUBATION PERIOD**

6½–13 weeks (longer at lower temperatures)

| weeks | 5 | 10 | 15 |

Loggerheads lay up to six clutches of eggs during the breeding season. The temperature of the sand determines whether the baby turtles are male or female. Cooler temperatures result in more males; if it's hotter, more females.

EGGS PER CLUTCH

UP TO
200

## Long-distance traveler

The loggerhead is the most widespread ocean-going turtle and uses its flippers to swim long distances. Helped by currents, loggerheads sometimes cross the Pacific, the world's biggest ocean.

"**Pregnant** lemon sharks **return** to the **same lagoon** to give birth every two years"

# HOMING SHARK
## LEMON SHARK

**The lemon shark finds safety** and comfort in a tropical lagoon. Dozens of pregnant lemon sharks gather to give birth at the Bimini Lagoon in the Bahamas, having returned to where they themselves were born years before. The babies have been nourished in the bodies of their mothers and after they are born they will stay in the warm shallows of the lagoon, using it as a nursery. Only when they are old enough will they join the grown-ups in deeper coastal waters.

## AT A GLANCE

- **SIZE** 8¼–9¾ ft (2.5–3 m) long

- **HABITAT** Shallow ocean waters, including coral reefs, mangrove fringes, and river mouths; may enter deeper ocean waters

- **LOCATION** Warm and tropical coastlines of America, the Caribbean, and western Africa

- **DIET** Mainly fish, including other sharks; young sharks also feed on crabs, shrimp, and octopuses

Yellowish body with no markings

## STATS AND FACTS

The young lemon sharks stay in the shallows of their nursery for up to eight years before they venture into deeper water.

### SWIMMING DEPTH

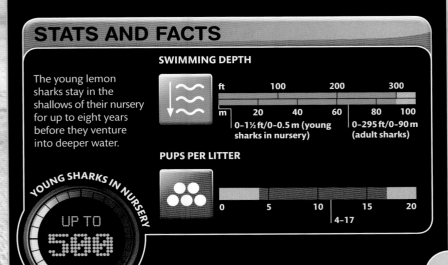

| ft | | 100 | 200 | 300 |
|---|---|---|---|---|
| m | 20 | 40 | 60 | 80 | 100 |

0–1½ ft/0–0.5 m (young sharks in nursery)

0–295 ft/0–90 m (adult sharks)

### PUPS PER LITTER

| | 0 | 5 | 10 | 15 | 20 |
|---|---|---|---|---|---|

4–17

YOUNG SHARKS IN NURSERY
UP TO
500

## LIFE IN A LAGOON

Warm shallow lagoons carpeted in white coral sand are a comfortable home for lemon sharks. Here there is plenty of food—in the form of fish straying from the nearby reef—and safety from danger.

# THE OCEAN GANG

Lemon sharks are very social creatures. In their first year, the young sharks grow up in the safety of a nursery. By the time they are two or three years old, they prefer to stay with same-sex groups of similar ages and spend much of their time in these gangs. Living in groups provides protection from bigger predators but it may also help sharks find food and a mate. These gangs often hang around fishing piers at night.

**ON THE OCEAN FLOOR**
The common tope prefers to hunt close to the bottom of its habitat. Pregnant females move to the shallower waters of estuaries and coastal bays to give birth.

# SHARK ON THE MOVE

## COMMON TOPE SHARK

**You will probably find a tope shark** in any ocean you care to visit: they are among the most wide ranging of all sharks and are happy in coastal shallows as well as the open ocean. They prefer low temperatures and move away from warm waters in hot summers—either toward the icy poles or down to cooler depths. They are strong swimmers and can cover great distances in a day. Some individuals can clock up journeys of thousands of miles during one of their migrations.

### AT A GLANCE

- **SIZE** 4½–6½ ft (1.35–2 m) long

- **HABITAT** Shallow coastal ocean waters, usually near the bottom

- **LOCATION** Cooler oceans outside the tropics, mainly near coastlines of continents and islands

- **DIET** Fish, squid, and octopus; young sharks also prey on shrimp, worms, and snails

### STATS AND FACTS

Some tope sharks live permanently near the equator, but move into deeper, cooler waters when it gets really hot.

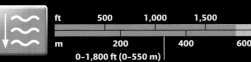

**DISTANCE**

35 miles/56 km (distance traveled per day)

| miles | 500 | 1,000 | 1,500 | |
|---|---|---|---|---|
| km | 1,000 | 2,000 | | 3,000 |

1,570 miles/2,525 km (max. recorded migration distance)

**SWIMMING DEPTH**

| ft | 500 | 1,000 | 1,500 | |
|---|---|---|---|---|
| m | 200 | 400 | | 600 |

0–1,800 ft (0–550 m)

MAX. LIFESPAN

"Tope sharks move **toward the poles** in summer and **the equator** in winter"

**OCEAN SHUT-EYE**

Short underwater naps keep a walrus going at sea. The tusks are canine teeth and are used for showing off to other walruses or for cutting air holes in ice.

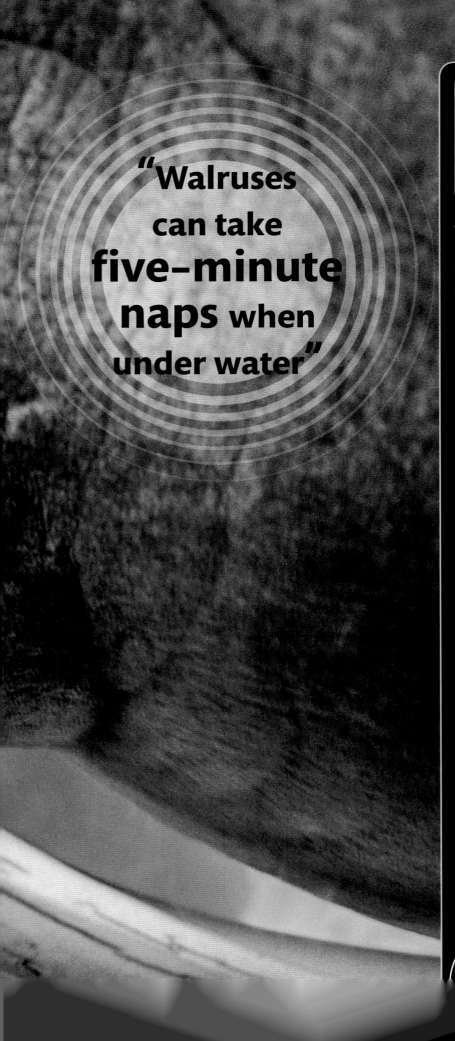

> "Walruses can take **five-minute naps** when under water"

# TUSKY DOZER
## WALRUS

**The walrus has one of the strange**st sleep patterns of any animal. In the frozen Arctic, on the top of the world, walruses live in icy water and can spend more than a week at a time on fishing expeditions. It means they have to doze whenever they get a chance, hanging off ice floes with their tusks or even when they are completely submerged. When they are especially busy, walruses can go for more than three days without any sleep at all. They make up for it when they return to land, when hundreds will snooze packed together on a favorite beach.

## AT A GLANCE

- **SIZE** 9¾–12 ft (3–3.6 m) long

- **HABITAT** Cold Arctic coastlines and on ice floes, diving in shallow marine waters

- **LOCATION** Region around the North Pole, southward as far as North Pacific islands and Greenland in the Atlantic

- **DIET** Mostly clams, but also worms, snails, shrimp, crabs, sea cucumbers, and slow-moving fish

## STATS AND FACTS

**84 HOURS**
MAX. TIME WITHOUT SLEEP

MAX. TIME ASLEEP

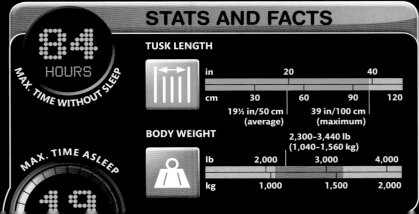

**TUSK LENGTH**

| in | | 20 | | 40 |
|---|---|---|---|---|
| cm | 30 | 60 | 90 | 120 |

19½ in/50 cm (average)    39 in/100 cm (maximum)

**BODY WEIGHT**

2,300–3,440 lb (1,040–1,560 kg)

| lb | 2,000 | 3,000 | 4,000 |
|---|---|---|---|
| kg | 1,000 | 1,500 | 2,000 |

# SEAFARING SERPENT

## SEA SNAKE

**Lots of the animals in the ocean** look like snakes, but real sea snakes are venomous reptiles that breathe air. This usually keeps them near the surface, although they can close their nostrils to dive deeper. They have a paddlelike tail to help them swim and most give birth to live young underwater—unlike other sea reptiles, they do not have to go to land to lay eggs. This makes them the only reptiles that spend their entire lives at sea.

## AT A GLANCE

- **SIZE** 2½–5 ft (0.75-1.5 m); a few species may grow bigger

- **HABITAT** Warm, shallow coastal ocean waters

- **LOCATION** Coastlines of the tropical Indian and Pacific Oceans, with greatest diversity around Australia

- **DIET** Mainly fish; some feed on specific types of fish, but only one species of sea snake is specialized for eating crustaceans and mollusks

## STATS AND FACTS

### SWIMMING DEPTH

| ft | | 150 | | 300 | |
|---|---|---|---|---|---|
| m | 40 | | 80 | | 120 |

330 ft/100 m (maximum)

### FANG LENGTH

| in | | ⅛ | | ¼ | |
|---|---|---|---|---|---|
| mm | 2 | | 4 | 6 | 8 |

½₂–⅛ in (0.6-4 mm)

**38** MAXIMUM LITTER SIZE

**2** MAX. TIME UNDER WATER

**BANDS FOR DANGER**
The striking banded pattern of a sea snake warns predators to keep away. Although many species are not aggressive, they all have strong venom, and some could kill a human.

"**One drop** of sea snake venom is enough to **kill three humans**"

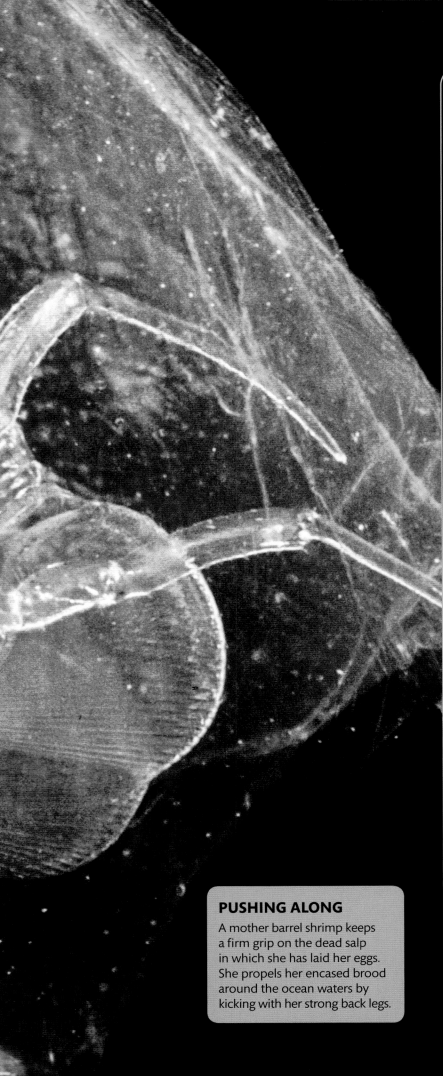

# MOBILE NURSERY
## BARREL SHRIMP

**Here is a shrimp** with a taste for flesh and a very gruesome family life. Most animal mothers in the open ocean scatter their eggs and leave it to chance whether their babies survive. But the mother barrel shrimp turns her prey into a stroller for her brood. First she catches a plump little jelly called a salp. She chomps away at its innards until the only thing left is its barrel-shaped skin. Then she lays her eggs inside this empty barrel and pushes it around wherever she goes until they hatch.

### AT A GLANCE

- **SIZE** ³⁄₁₆–1½ in (5–42 mm)
- **HABITAT** Deep sea
- **LOCATION** Worldwide
- **DIET** Salps (floating jellylike animals) and other soft-bodied animal plankton

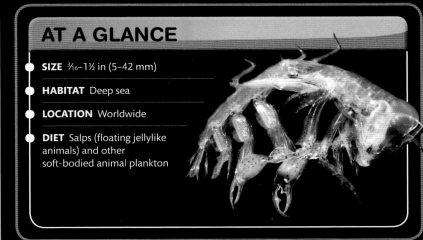

### STATS AND FACTS

Barrel shrimp lay their eggs in prey soft enough to scrape out. Salps are favorite targets, but sometimes they attack tiny jellyfish and similar animals.

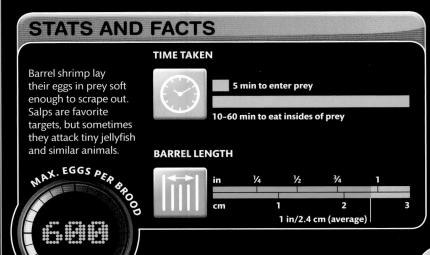

**TIME TAKEN**

5 min to enter prey

10–60 min to eat insides of prey

**MAX. EGGS PER BROOD**

600

**BARREL LENGTH**

| in | ¼ | ½ | ¾ | 1 |
|---|---|---|---|---|
| cm | 1 | 2 | | 3 |

1 in/2.4 cm (average)

### PUSHING ALONG

A mother barrel shrimp keeps a firm grip on the dead salp in which she has laid her eggs. She propels her encased brood around the ocean waters by kicking with her strong back legs.

"Young catsharks use their **rough skin** to **tear food** apart"

# CAT-EYED NIGHT PROWLER
## SMALL SPOTTED CATSHARK

**Hunting in the dark is no problem** for this little shark. Its sensitive eyes help it prowl the seas of Europe, where it snaps at small animals that live close to the sandy and muddy bottoms of coastal waters. It is one of the most abundant sharks in European waters and eats whatever its jaws can tackle—including fish, crabs, and squid. The small spotted catshark is active mostly at night and spends the day resting motionless under craggy rocks or elsewhere on the sea floor.

## AT A GLANCE

- **SIZE** 31–39 in (80–100 cm) long
- **HABITAT** Coastal ocean waters
- **LOCATION** Northeast Atlantic Ocean and Mediterranean Sea
- **DIET** Fish, worms, shrimp, and snails

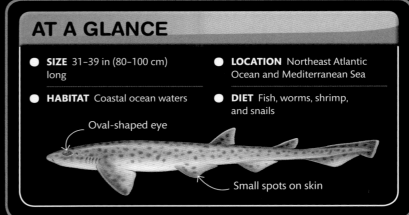

Oval-shaped eye

Small spots on skin

## STATS AND FACTS

**EYE DIAMETER**

Although the eyes of a catshark are not especially big, they are good for nighttime hunting.

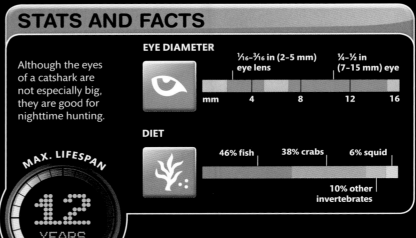

$\frac{1}{16}$–$\frac{3}{16}$ in (2–5 mm) eye lens

$\frac{1}{4}$–$\frac{1}{2}$ in (7–15 mm) eye

| mm | 4 | 8 | 12 | 16 |

**DIET**

46% fish | 38% crabs | 6% squid

10% other invertebrates

**MAX. LIFESPAN**

**12 YEARS**

### SLEEK HUNTER
Most types of catsharks have a slender body and skin that is patterned with spots or other markings. They are named for their oval catlike eyes that are positioned high on their head.

"They are **too slow** to catch swimming seals, so they take **sleeping** ones instead"

# SLOW MOVER
## GREENLAND SHARK

**Life slows down in the ice-cold waters** of the Arctic, and the Greenland shark is probably the slowest giant fish in the ocean. It can manage only half the cruising speed of a seal and it takes a full seven seconds just to sweep its tail from one side to the other. As a result, the Greenland shark cannot chase down its prey. Instead, it relies on creeping up on its victims and taking them by surprise. Amazingly, this is good enough to grab an unsuspecting seal—or even a seabird.

## AT A GLANCE

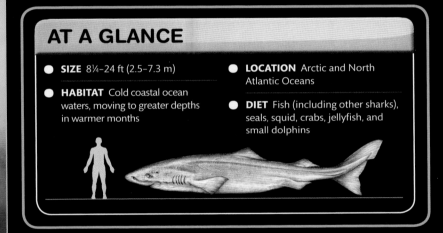

- **SIZE** 8¼–24 ft (2.5–7.3 m)

- **HABITAT** Cold coastal ocean waters, moving to greater depths in warmer months

- **LOCATION** Arctic and North Atlantic Oceans

- **DIET** Fish (including other sharks), seals, squid, crabs, jellyfish, and small dolphins

## STATS AND FACTS

Sharks develop slowly when they remain in cold waters. The Greenland shark grows nearly a hundred times slower than certain speedy sharks that live in the tropics.

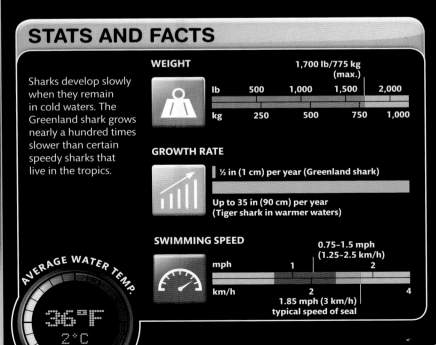

**WEIGHT** 1,700 lb/775 kg (max.)

| lb | 500 | 1,000 | 1,500 | 2,000 |
|---|---|---|---|---|
| kg | 250 | 500 | 750 | 1,000 |

**GROWTH RATE**

½ in (1 cm) per year (Greenland shark)

Up to 35 in (90 cm) per year (Tiger shark in warmer waters)

**SWIMMING SPEED**

0.75–1.5 mph (1.25–2.5 km/h)

| mph | | 1 | | 2 | |
|---|---|---|---|---|---|
| km/h | | | 2 | | 4 |

1.85 mph (3 km/h) typical speed of seal

AVERAGE WATER TEMP.
**36°F**
**2°C**

### GIANT SCAVENGER

The Greenland shark gets meat where it can, and sometimes it scavenges dead animals it finds in shallow waters. Some sharks have even been found with the remains of reindeer in their stomach.

# SLIMY COCOON CRAFTER
## PARROTFISH

**The parrotfish makes the most** of the coral reef—getting not just food from this ocean habitat but shelter too. It gnaws away at the coral with a sharp parrotlike beak. The soft living parts of the coral are nutritious, but the rocky parts pass out of its body as sand. At night the parrotfish sleeps in a safe crevice. Here, some species release a special kind of slime from their mouth and use it for making their bed. They spread it out like a blanket until it covers their entire body in an underwater cocoon as extra protection against predators.

### AT A GLANCE

- **SIZE** 1–4¼ ft (0.3–1.3 m) long, depending on the species
- **HABITAT** Shallow ocean waters and coral reefs
- **LOCATION** Worldwide, but especially in the tropics
- **DIET** Coral and algae

### STATS AND FACTS

**WEIGHT OF CORAL CONSUMED**

| oz | 4 | 8 |
|---|---|---|
| g | 100 | 200 | 300 |

9¾ oz/275 g (per day)

The crumbled coral eaten by parrotfish contains nutritious algae, but the hard rock passes through their bodies.

**BITES OF CORAL PER MINUTE**

0   10   20   30   40

1–35 (less for big fish, more for smaller fish)

**TIME TO BUILD COCOON**

45–60 MIN

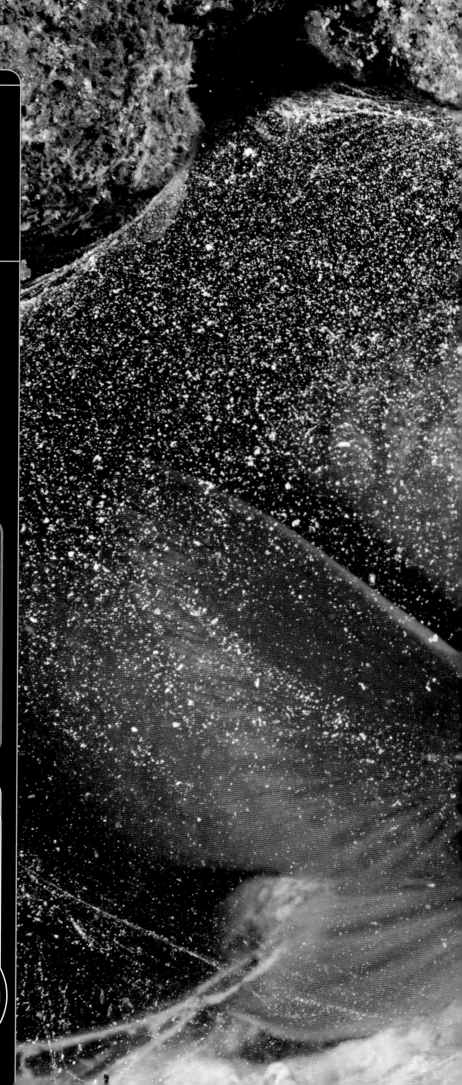

**SLIMY SCREEN**

A cocoon made from slime hides a parrotfish from predators. It also protects a sleeping fish from ocean bugs, such as fish lice, that could infect its body at night.

# HOME LOVER
## BLACKTIP REEF SHARK

**A tropical coral reef is so packed with life** that a hungry shark does not have to go far in its search for a meal. The blacktip reef shark is a common predator on the reefs of tropical Asia and Australasia—but it sticks to hunting on a patch that is sometimes only twice the area of a soccer field. It can stay near its favorite reef for years on end. Only pregnant females move away from the reef when they are about to give birth.

### AT A GLANCE

- **SIZE** 3¼–6½ ft (1–2 m) long
- **HABITAT** Shallow tropical ocean waters, especially on coral reefs
- **LOCATION** Indian Ocean and western Pacific Ocean
- **DIET** Fish, squid, shrimp, and snails

## STATS AND FACTS

**AVERAGE HOME RANGE**

| sq miles | 0.1 | 0.2 |
| --- | --- | --- |
| sq km | 0.2 | 0.4 | 0.6 | 0.8 |

0.08–0.2 sq miles (0.3–0.7 sq km)

**AREA OF HUNTING PATCH**

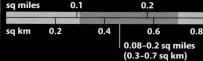

| sq miles | 0.1 | 0.2 |
| --- | --- | --- |
| sq km | 0.2 | 0.4 | 0.6 | 0.8 |

0.003–0.03 sq miles (0.009–0.13 sq km)

**SWIMMING DEPTH**

0–245 ft/0–75 m (adults)

| ft | 100 | 200 |
| --- | --- | --- |
| m | 20 | 40 | 60 | 80 |

0–9¾ ft/0–3 m (young)

Young blacktip reef sharks stay in shallow lagoons but move into deeper waters as they grow older. Even as adults, they spend most of their time patrolling a territory that is a hundred times smaller than the entire reef, following their prey from one tiny hunting patch to another.

**BLACK-MARKED SHARK**
The bold, black markings on the tip of its tail and fins make this shark one of the most distinctive reef sharks. Its dorsal fin is often seen sticking up out of the water.

# LAGOON RAIDERS

In warm lagoons, hungry blacktip reef sharks are drawn to dense schools of fish. Typically, only young sharks are found in such shallow waters but here adult sharks are working together to herd the schools. The sharks push the schools ever closer to the shoreline where the fish bunch into tighter groups. When they think the prey is crowded enough for a good mouthful, the sharks lunge in for a bite.

"**Blacktip reef sharks often swim** in water that is **only 1 ft** (30 cm) **deep**"

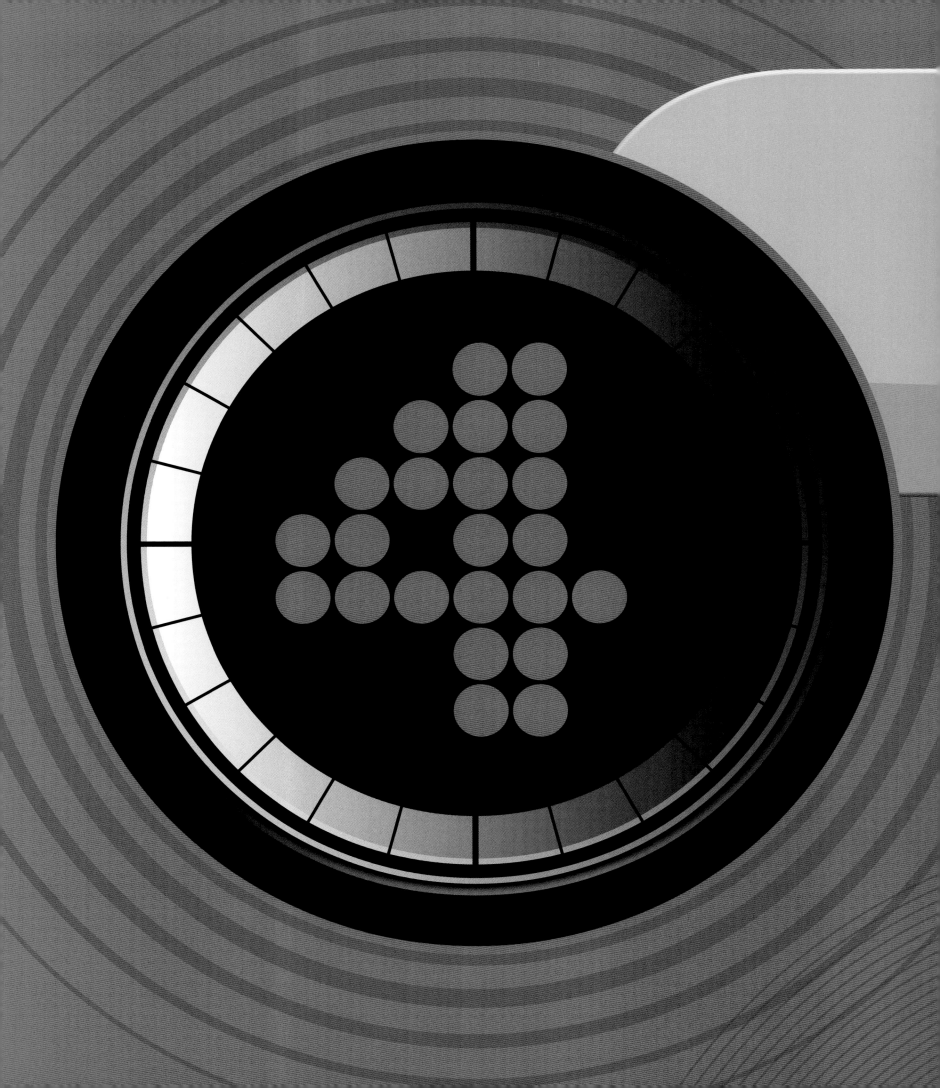

# SUPERNATURAL SENSES

Competition is fierce in the ocean, so it helps if you have a little extra something that gives you an advantage over another species. Whether it is extraordinary eyesight, a nose for trouble, or downright sneaky behavior, the tactics some marine animals deploy are truly amazing.

# WIDE-EYED SENSATION
## HAMMERHEAD

**It is hard to imagine what the world looks like** when you have as wide a view of it as a hammerhead shark. However, excellent vision is only one part of the hammerhead's story. Its extraordinary head is also packed with sensors and sweeping it from side to side helps the shark find prey. It may even be useful in helping the shark stay buoyant while swimming.

Large olfactory sac is excellent at picking up smells

Long optic nerve carries information about vision from the eye to the brain

Shark makes a grab for prey

## AT A GLANCE

- **SIZE** 11¾–20 ft (3.6–6.1 m)
- **HABITAT** Oceans near land, but especially over coral reefs
- **LOCATION** Worldwide in tropical and warm waters
- **DIET** Many fish, but especially stingrays, groupers, and catfish

## STATS AND FACTS

### HEAD WIDTH

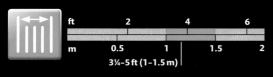

| ft | | 2 | | 4 | | 6 |
|----|--|---|--|---|--|---|
| m | 0.5 | 1 | | 1.5 | | 2 |

3¼–5 ft (1–1.5 m)

Nearly a dozen species of hammerheads, all with different hammer shapes and sizes, are found around the world. Some travel long distances on their migrations.

### MIGRATION DISTANCE

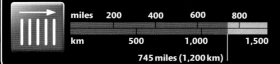

| miles | 200 | 400 | 600 | 800 |
|-------|-----|-----|-----|-----|
| km | 500 | 1,000 | 1,500 | |

745 miles (1,200 km)

MAX. SENSORY PORES

3,000

### FINDING BURIED FOOD

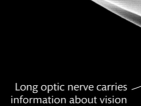

The shark sweeps its head from side to side like a metal detector so that the front edge of its hammer picks up signals coming from its favorite buried prey—stingrays.

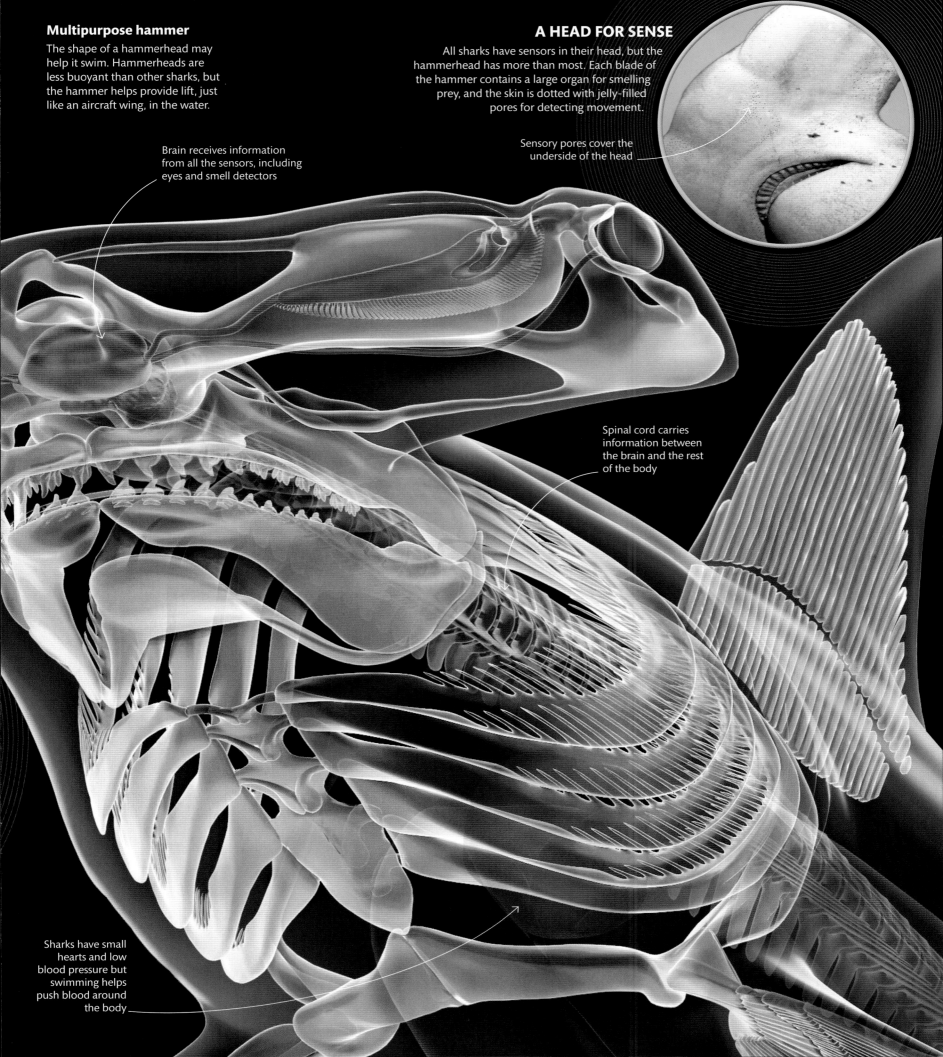

**Multipurpose hammer**
The shape of a hammerhead may help it swim. Hammerheads are less buoyant than other sharks, but the hammer helps provide lift, just like an aircraft wing, in the water.

**A HEAD FOR SENSE**
All sharks have sensors in their head, but the hammerhead has more than most. Each blade of the hammer contains a large organ for smelling prey, and the skin is dotted with jelly-filled pores for detecting movement.

Sensory pores cover the underside of the head

Brain receives information from all the sensors, including eyes and smell detectors

Spinal cord carries information between the brain and the rest of the body

Sharks have small hearts and low blood pressure but swimming helps push blood around the body

## KNOCKING HAMMERHEADS

Scalloped hammerheads form some of
the biggest schools, or "shivers," of sharks
anywhere in the ocean, often with hundreds
of fish gathered together in one place. These
schools swim close to shore during the day,
but move into deeper water to hunt at night.
The biggest ones are made up of younger
males or females. Individuals sometimes
knock one another with their snouts—perhaps
as signals of aggression or courtship.

# SENSORY WEAPON

## SAWSHARK

**An effective hunter needs to have an advantage** over its prey, such as excellent predatory senses or a vicious weapon. The sawshark has both. Its snout is drawn out into a long, sawlike beak, equipped with sensitive skin and feelers for probing its surroundings. When the sawshark senses a small fish or crab on the muddy ocean floor, it slashes from side to side until the teeth on its beak cripple the prey.

### AT A GLANCE

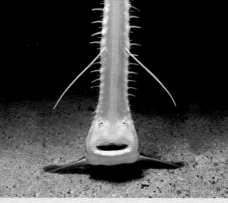

- **SIZE** 24–67 in (62–170 cm) long

- **HABITAT** Coastal ocean waters, usually near the sea floor

- **LOCATION** Bahamas, southern Africa, and western Pacific from Japan to Australia

- **DIET** Small fish, crabs, squid, and shrimp

## STATS AND FACTS

The "saw" of a sawshark is actually an extension of its snout. The skin is covered with the same kinds of sensory pores that are found on the snouts of other types of sharks.

**LENGTH OF "SAW"**

| in | | 5 | | 10 | | 15 |
|---|---|---|---|---|---|---|
| cm | 10 | 20 | | 30 | | 40 |

4¾–14 in (12–35 cm)

**LENGTH OF FEELERS**

| in | | 2 | | 4 | | 6 | |
|---|---|---|---|---|---|---|---|
| cm | 5 | | 10 | | 15 | | 20 |

2¼–6¼ in (6–16 cm)

**SWIMMING DEPTH**   3,280 ft/1,000 m (max. for Bahamas sawshark)

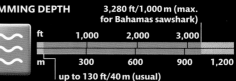

| ft | | 1,000 | | 2,000 | | 3,000 | |
|---|---|---|---|---|---|---|---|
| m | 300 | | 600 | | 900 | | 1,200 |

up to 130 ft/40 m (usual)

**MAX. TEETH ON SAW**

Snout extends into long beaklike "saw"

Sideways pointing teeth for slashing prey

Barbel, or feeler, is sensitive to touch and taste

### Feeling for food

The sensory feelers that hang down from either side of a sawshark's snout are sensitive to touch and pressure. They can even taste the presence of prey in the mud and sand on the ocean floor.

# BRAINIEST MOLLUSK
## BROADCLUB CUTTLEFISH

**The cuttlefish is a distant relation** of snails and slugs, but it may have best brainpower of any animal without a backbone. Its closest cousins are the squid and octopus and, like them, it has arms for grabbing food, and eyes that work as well as our own. The cuttlefish's brain is especially big—possibly to help it control color changes in its skin that signal its fear, excitement, or temper.

Large eyes have unusual W-shaped pupil

Suckers on arms and tentacles for grasping prey

Siphon squirts dark ink into water to distract predators

Flapping "skirt" along body works like a fin to help the cuttlefish swim

### Ocean chameleon
The cuttlefish's body contains a hard, air-packed cuttlebone for support and buoyancy. Its skin is dotted with tiny sacs of pigment that expand to make its surface change color.

## AT A GLANCE

- **SIZE** 6–20 in (15–50 cm) in body length
- **HABITAT** Ocean waters near coastlines, swimming mainly near the bottom over rocks or sand, or among seaweed
- **LOCATION** Worldwide
- **DIET** A wide range of invertebrates and fish

## STATS AND FACTS

**SACS OF SKIN PIGMENT**

| | | | 133,000 per sq in (20,000 per sq cm) |
|---|---|---|---|
| sq in | 50,000 | 100,000 | 150,000 |
| sq cm | 10,000 | 20,000 | 30,000 |

**5**
PIGMENT TYPES IN SKIN

**PROPORTION OF BRAIN USED FOR LEARNING**

24% (cuttlefish)

13% (octopus)

LIFESPAN

18-24 MONTHS

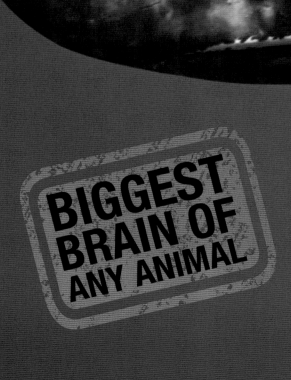

**BIGGEST BRAIN OF** ANY ANIMAL

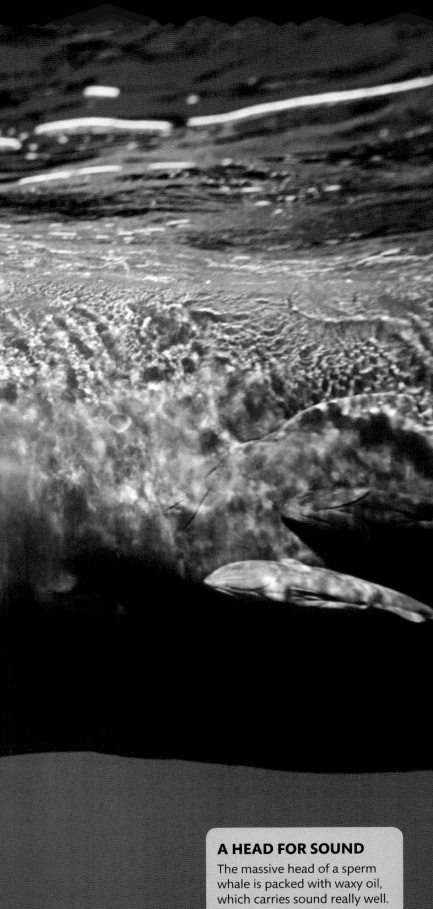

# BRAINY COLOSSUS
## SPERM WHALE

**The sperm whale is the world's** largest predator. Its jaw is longer than a car and each tooth is bigger than an ice cream cone. Sperm whales dive very deep in the ocean to prey on giant squid. Like all hunters, a sperm whale needs to be clever to catch its prey. Not even the blue whale—the biggest animal of all—has a larger brain.

### AT A GLANCE

- **SIZE** 36–66 ft (11–20 m) long; mature males can be twice as long as females
- **HABITAT** Open sea
- **LOCATION** Worldwide, in deep ocean waters, except those covered by ice
- **DIET** Mainly squid (including giant and colossal squid), but sometimes deep-sea octopuses and fish

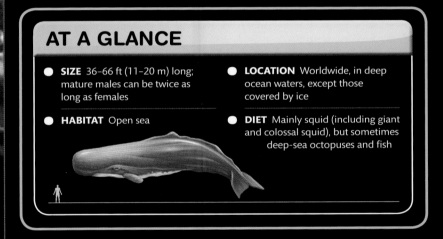

### STATS AND FACTS

**70 YEARS LIFESPAN**

Few air-breathing animals can hold their breath for as long as a sperm whale. By diving deeper and longer, sperm whales can find more prey.

**MAXIMUM WEIGHT**

| tons | | 20 | | 40 | | 60 | |
|------|---|----|---|----|---|----|---|
| tonnes | | 25 | | 50 | | | 75 |

63 tons (57 tonnes)

**AVERAGE BRAIN WEIGHT**    17 lb/7.8 kg (whale brain)

| lb | | 5 | 10 | 15 | 20 |
|----|---|---|----|----|----|
| kg | 2.5 | 5 | 7.5 | 10 |

3 lb/1.4 kg (human brain)

**DIVING DEPTH**    7,380 ft/ 2,250 m (max.)

| ft | | 3,000 | 6,000 | 9,000 |
|----|---|-------|-------|-------|
| m | 1,000 | 2,000 | 3,000 |

1,300 ft/400 m (usual)

**MAX. DIVE DURATION**

**90**

### A HEAD FOR SOUND

The massive head of a sperm whale is packed with waxy oil, which carries sound really well. This helps the sperm whale

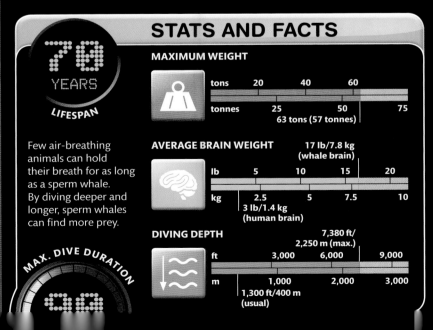

# HUNTER IN THE DARK
## TIGER SHARK

**Few animals can match the tiger shark's appetite.** Turtles, birds, other sharks, and even human beings, injured whales, and old tin cans all get gobbled down if it gets the chance. This fierce predator prowls around shorelines at night, often venturing into estuaries and harbors in search of food. It is usually alone and is perfectly at home hunting in dark and murky waters.

### AT A GLANCE

- **SIZE** 9¾–20 ft (3–6 m)

- **HABITAT** Usually in cloudy waters near coastlines, especially around estuaries, lagoons, and harbors

- **LOCATION** Worldwide in warm and tropical oceans

- **DIET** Fish, including other sharks, turtles, seals, seabirds, dolphins, sea snakes, squid, crabs, lobsters, snails, jellyfish, and human rubbish

### STAYING AFLOAT

A tiger shark has a large liver that sits on top of its stomach and gut. The liver contains a lot of oil, which helps the shark float and stay buoyant when swimming. It also has a spiral valve in its gut that slows down the passage of food so that it can absorb as many nutrients as possible.

Liver

Stomach

Spiral valve in gut

Young tigers have vertical stripes and spots that run down the length of the body and fade as the shark grows

Upper lobe of tail fin is bigger than lower lobe

### Guzzle guts

The tiger shark has a reputation of eating anything it comes across. This strategy is useful when there is not much food around, but it does mean that it sometimes swallows objects that it cannot digest. Like most sharks, it has a short gut, so bones and other hard materials have to stay in the stomach much longer or be vomited back up.

Anal fin keeps fish stable while swimming

Pelvic fins help fish move up and down and stop quickly

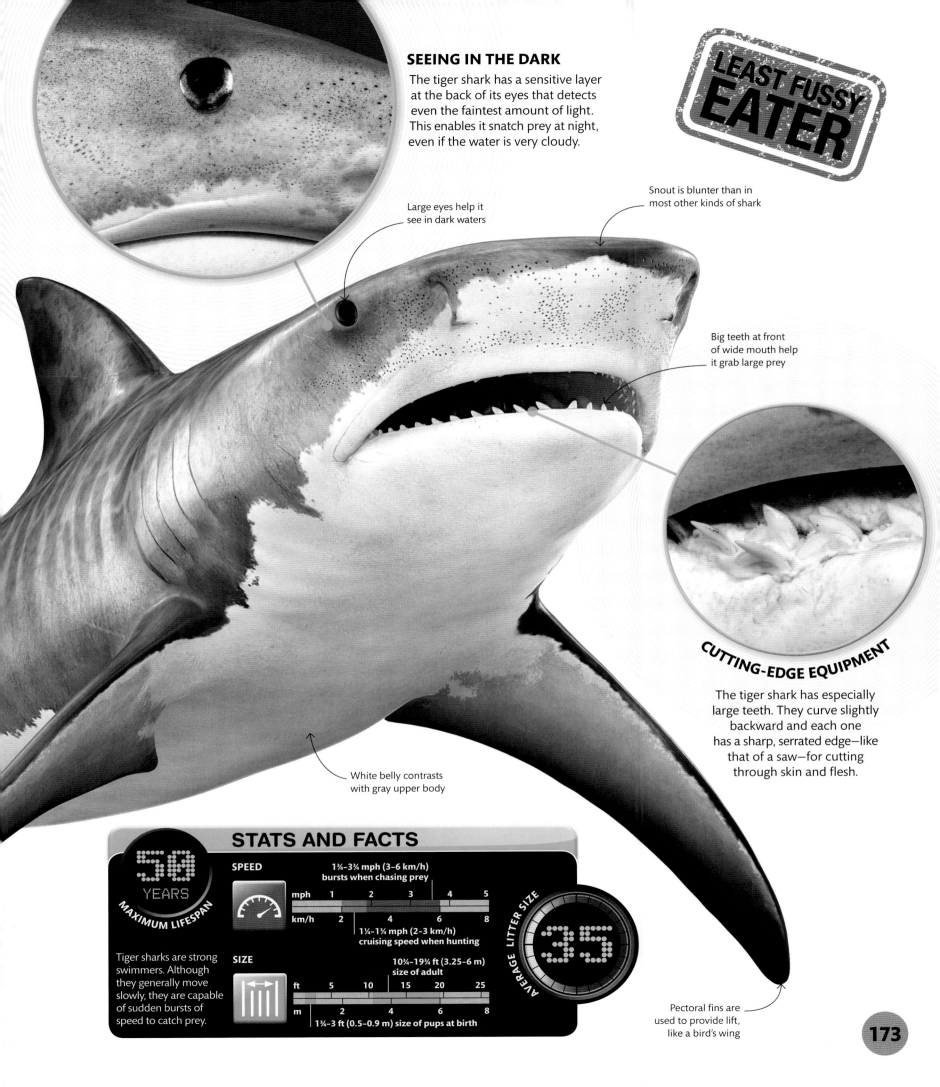

## SEEING IN THE DARK

The tiger shark has a sensitive layer at the back of its eyes that detects even the faintest amount of light. This enables it snatch prey at night, even if the water is very cloudy.

LEAST FUSSY EATER

Large eyes help it see in dark waters

Snout is blunter than in most other kinds of shark

Big teeth at front of wide mouth help it grab large prey

## CUTTING-EDGE EQUIPMENT

The tiger shark has especially large teeth. They curve slightly backward and each one has a sharp, serrated edge—like that of a saw—for cutting through skin and flesh.

White belly contrasts with gray upper body

## STATS AND FACTS

**58 YEARS**
MAXIMUM LIFESPAN

Tiger sharks are strong swimmers. Although they generally move slowly, they are capable of sudden bursts of speed to catch prey.

**SPEED**

1¾–3¾ mph (3–6 km/h) bursts when chasing prey

| mph | 1 | 2 | 3 | 4 | 5 |
|-----|---|---|---|---|---|
| km/h | 2 | 4 | 6 | 8 |

1¼–1¾ mph (2–3 km/h) cruising speed when hunting

**SIZE**

10¾–19¾ ft (3.25–6 m) size of adult

| ft | 5 | 10 | 15 | 20 | 25 |
|----|---|----|----|----|----|
| m | 2 | 4 | 6 | 8 |

1¾–3 ft (0.5–0.9 m) size of pups at birth

**35**
AVERAGE LITTER SIZE

Pectoral fins are used to provide lift, like a bird's wing

"Tiger sharks **eat more humans** than **great white** sharks"

## SAFETY FIRST

Many sharks rely on vision for hunting, so they need to protect their eyes when attacking prey—even a little fish can inflict a painful slap. At the moment this tiger shark attacks, it automatically blinks a protective membrane over its eyes to prevent the flailing prey from causing damage. Many other species of sharks lack this membrane. Instead, they roll their eyes backward in their sockets when they lunge for their prey.

## EYE BANDS

The bands across a mantis shrimp's eye are actually rows of sensors. Different types of sensors are able to detect movement and different colors—as well as some kinds of light that are invisible to us.

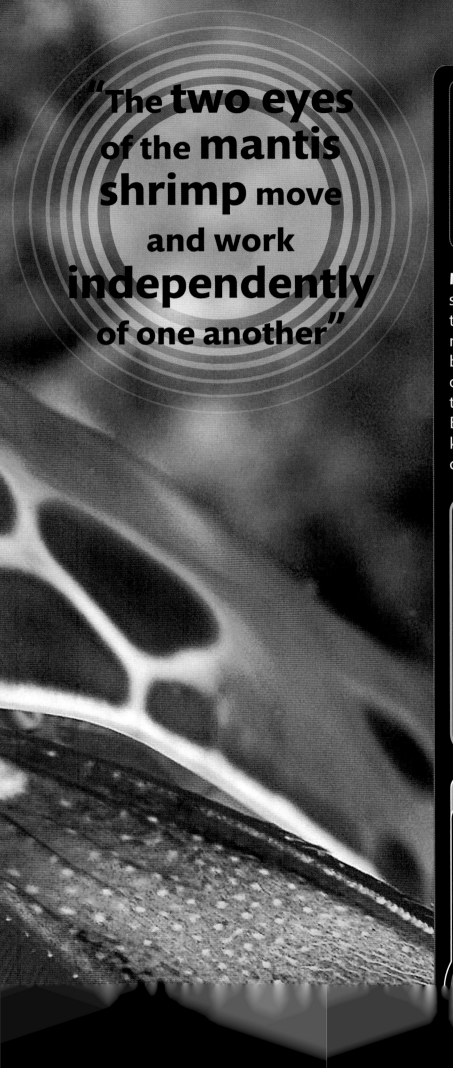

"The **two eyes** of the **mantis shrimp** move and work **independently** of one another"

# EXTRAORDINARY EYES
## MANTIS SHRIMP

**Mantis shrimp need good eyesight**. They smash or spear their prey with lightning-fast claws so they have to be a good judge of distance to get a direct hit and make a kill. Things could easily become confusing in the bright and shimmering world of a tropical reef filled with color and shining surfaces. Some creatures even have transparent shells, making them more difficult to spot. But the mantis shrimp's eyes have so many different kinds of sensors to cope with these challenges that it can see everything clearly.

## AT A GLANCE

- **SIZE** Up to 14 in (35 cm) long, depending on the species
- **HABITAT** Muddy, sandy, and gravelly ocean floors and coral reefs, in shallow coastal waters
- **LOCATION** Worldwide, with more species in the tropics
- **DIET** Snails, fish, crabs, and shrimp

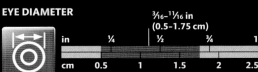

## STATS AND FACTS

Different kinds of eye sensors can detect different colors. Mantis shrimps have four times as many sensors as humans.

### VISION

| 12 color receptors (mantis shrimp) | | | |
|---|---|---|---|
| 0 | 5 | 10 | 15 |

3 receptors (human)

### EYE DIAMETER

³⁄₁₆–¹¹⁄₁₆ in (0.5–1.75 cm)

| in | ¼ | ½ | ¾ | 1 |
|---|---|---|---|---|
| cm | 0.5 | 1 | 1.5 | 2 | 2.5 |

ROTATION OF EYES

# SNEAKY KILLER
## BROADNOSE SEVENGILL SHARK

**In coastal ocean waters** close to where muddy rivers run into the sea, conditions can get very murky. This makes it difficult for many ocean-going predators to hunt their prey—but not this one. The broadnose sevengill shark loves this habitat: it is just right for sneaking up on prey without being seen. This shark hunts large prey, including dolphins and other sharks. It does not have the stamina for long chases, so it gets as close to its victim as it can before attacking from behind with a quick burst of speed. Sometimes several sharks work together during a hunt to take their prey by surprise.

"This shark **pokes its head** out of the water to **find prey** near the surface"

## AT A GLANCE

- **SIZE** 7¼–9¾ ft (2.2–3 m) long
- **HABITAT** Coastal ocean waters, bays, and estuaries, often in cloudy water
- **LOCATION** Coastlines of western North America, South America, South Africa, and the western Pacific Ocean
- **DIET** Fish, including other sharks, seals, dolphins, and carrion

## STATS AND FACTS

**SPEED**

5–22 km/h (3–13½ mph) hunting speed

| mph | 5 | 10 | 15 |
|---|---|---|---|

| km/h | 5 | 10 | 15 | 20 | 25 |
|---|---|---|---|---|---|

1.7 km/h (1 mph) cruising speed

This shark spends much of its time cruising slowly, but it can move fast to attack its prey.

**SWIMMING DEPTH**

| ft | 500 | 1,000 | 1,500 |
|---|---|---|---|

| m | 200 | 400 | 600 |
|---|---|---|---|

0–570 m (0–1,870 ft)

EST. MAXIMUM LIFESPAN

50

**BLENDING IN**

The gray upper body of the broadnose sevengill shark helps it blend into the cloudy waters of its favorite hunting grounds. Unlike most other sharks, which have five gill slits, this shark has seven.

# SHOCK TACTICS
## TORPEDO RAY

**The torpedo ray looks like a harmless flatfish** but it has a stunning secret weapon. Its fleshy body is packed with a pair of fat electrical organs that can fire a shock through the surrounding seawater. The ray uses its organs to electrocute its fishy prey—but, if provoked, it is more than willing to use them when danger threatens.

## AT A GLANCE

- **SIZE** 20–70 in (50–180 cm) long; 12–39¼ in (30–100 cm) in diameter

- **HABITAT** Open ocean waters or near coastlines. Young rays live in shallower waters on sand, mud, or coral reefs

- **LOCATION** Worldwide in warm and tropical oceans

- **DIET** Small fish

Kidney-shaped electrical organ

Pectoral fins are winglike and surround the body to form a flat, disklike shape

## ELECTROCUTING ENEMIES

If something grabs its tail, the torpedo ray arches its back and curls its white belly outward toward its attacker. The shock will then hit the attacker in the face.

Curling its body enables the ray to produce an outward rather than a downward shock

### Simply stunning

The electric organs of the torpedo ray are under the direct control of the ray's brain. When the ray spots an unsuspecting fish, it gently hovers over it before zapping it with an electric shock. As it delivers the shock, the ray wraps itself around its victim. The stunned fish is then swallowed whole.

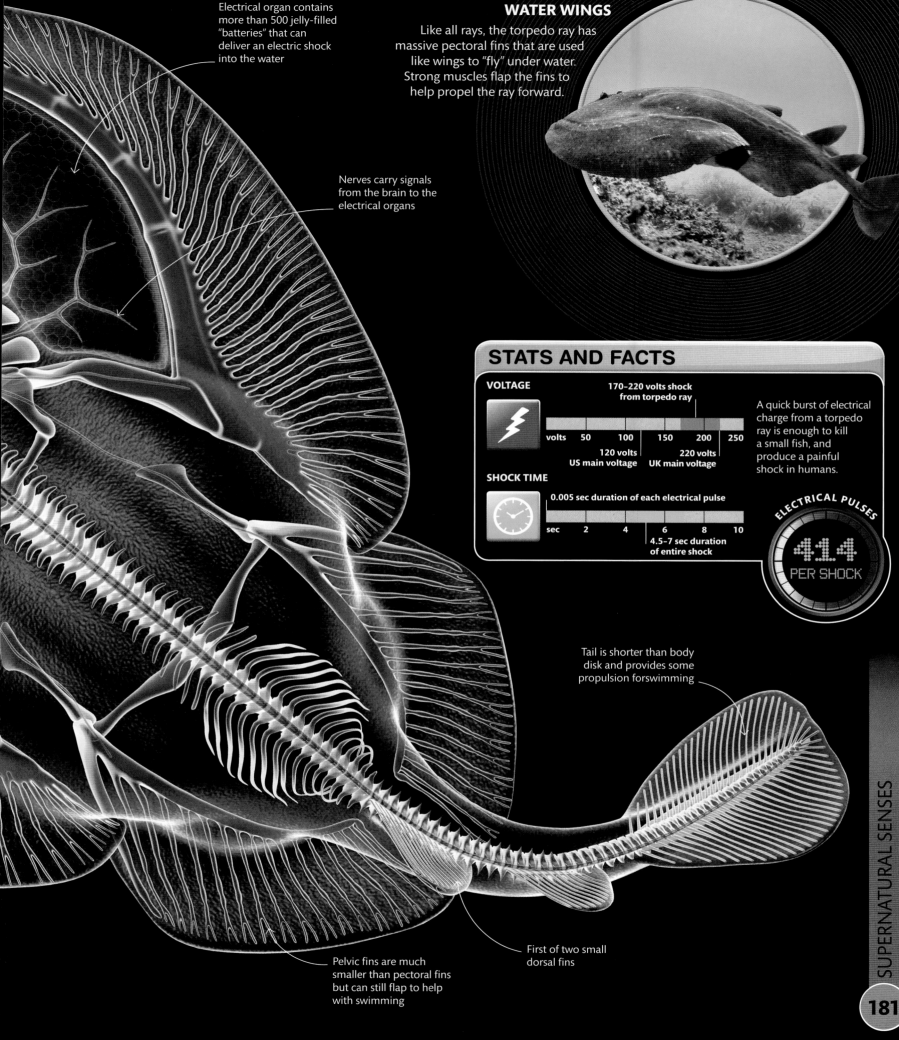

Electrical organ contains more than 500 jelly-filled "batteries" that can deliver an electric shock into the water

Nerves carry signals from the brain to the electrical organs

**WATER WINGS**

Like all rays, the torpedo ray has massive pectoral fins that are used like wings to "fly" under water. Strong muscles flap the fins to help propel the ray forward.

## STATS AND FACTS

**VOLTAGE**

170–220 volts shock from torpedo ray

| volts | 50 | 100 | 150 | 200 | 250 |
|---|---|---|---|---|---|

120 volts
US main voltage

220 volts
UK main voltage

A quick burst of electrical charge from a torpedo ray is enough to kill a small fish, and produce a painful shock in humans.

**SHOCK TIME**

0.005 sec duration of each electrical pulse

| sec | 2 | 4 | 6 | 8 | 10 |
|---|---|---|---|---|---|

4.5–7 sec duration of entire shock

ELECTRICAL PULSES

**414**

PER SHOCK

Tail is shorter than body disk and provides some propulsion forswimming

Pelvic fins are much smaller than pectoral fins but can still flap to help with swimming

First of two small dorsal fins

**WAITING FOR A KILL**
Sandtiger sharks not only cooperate to make their hunting more effective, but can hover motionless in the water. They do this by gulping air at the surface to make their bodies more buoyant.

# DEADLY SCHOOL
## SANDTIGER SHARK

**Sharks gather whenever there is the prospect** of food, but sandtiger sharks often work together to make the most of a feeding opportunity. A number of sandtigers swim around a school of fish until it is surrounded. Then they move in closer so that the prey bunches together. By the time the sharks dive in for a kill, they are sure to grab a good mouthful of fish. They also snack on other sharks and rays that come too close.

## AT A GLANCE

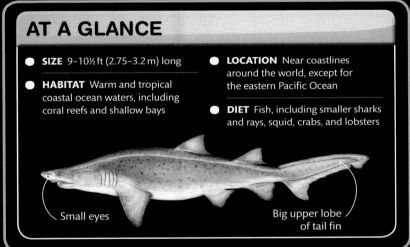

- **SIZE** 9–10½ ft (2.75–3.2 m) long
- **HABITAT** Warm and tropical coastal ocean waters, including coral reefs and shallow bays
- **LOCATION** Near coastlines around the world, except for the eastern Pacific Ocean
- **DIET** Fish, including smaller sharks and rays, squid, crabs, and lobsters

Small eyes

Big upper lobe of tail fin

## STATS AND FACTS

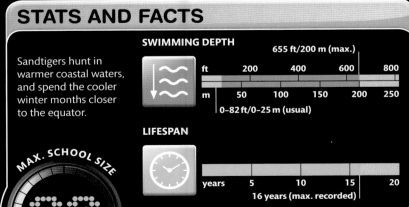

Sandtigers hunt in warmer coastal waters, and spend the cooler winter months closer to the equator.

**SWIMMING DEPTH**

655 ft/200 m (max.)

| ft | 200 | 400 | 600 | 800 |
|----|-----|-----|-----|-----|
| m | 50 | 100 | 150 | 200 | 250 |

0–82 ft/0–25 m (usual)

**LIFESPAN**

| years | 5 | 10 | 15 | 20 |
|-------|---|----|----|----|

16 years (max. recorded)

MAX. SCHOOL SIZE

"Although they look **fierce**, sandtigers prefer to **stay away** from **humans**"

## SCARY SMILER

The sandtiger shark has one of the toothiest grins of any shark and a distinctly menacing look. Its teeth project forward and the shark swims with its mouth slightly open. Some sandtiger sharks have tiny animals called hydroids growing on their teeth. This probably happens when they have gone for a long period of time without feeding. Some scientists think that female sandtigers stop hunting while they are pregnant.

# WIRED FOR SOUND
## SILKY SHARK

**It can be difficult to find a decent meal** in the wide expanse of the open ocean. However, silky sharks can pick up low-pitched sounds and are especially good at detecting rumbles that are deeper than a bass drum. In the ocean these may signal that a feeding frenzy is nearby: rumbling sounds are made when lots of sharks gather at a kill and frantically chase and snap at their prey. Many sharks sense blood in the water—but silky sharks are also drawn to the sounds of other sharks eating, so they can get a share of the meal.

## AT A GLANCE

- **SIZE** 7½–11 ft (2.3–3.3 m) long
- **HABITAT** Warm waters, mainly of the open ocean, often near islands; younger sharks occur in more coastal waters
- **LOCATION** Worldwide in tropical oceans
- **DIET** Fish and squid

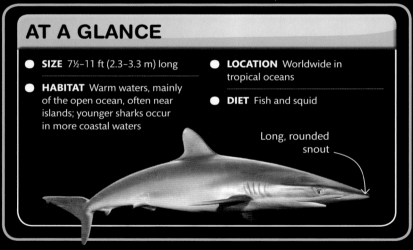

Long, rounded snout

## STATS AND FACTS

**HEARING RANGE** 10–1,000 Hz (silky shark)

| Hz | 5,000 | 10,000 | 15,000 | 20,000 |
|---|---|---|---|---|

| Hz | 5,000 | 10,000 | 15,000 | 20,000 |
|---|---|---|---|---|

20–20,000 Hz (human)

Silky sharks can hear lower pitched (deeper) sounds than humans, which is why they are so good at using sound to hunt in the ocean.

**SOUND DETECTION DISTANCE**

| ft | 400 | 800 | 1,200 | 1,800 |
|---|---|---|---|---|

| m | 100 | 200 | 300 | 400 | 500 |
|---|---|---|---|---|---|

max. 410–1,310 ft (125–400 m)

PITCH MOST ATTRACTED TO

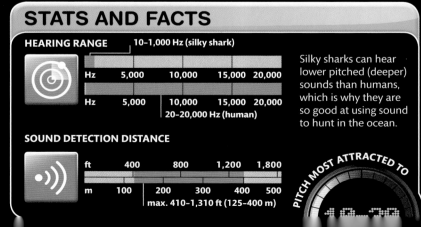

**SMOOTH SWIMMER**

Silky sharks get their name from their smooth skin. The prickles that make the skin of other sharks so rough are tinier and more closely packed on the skin of a silky shark.

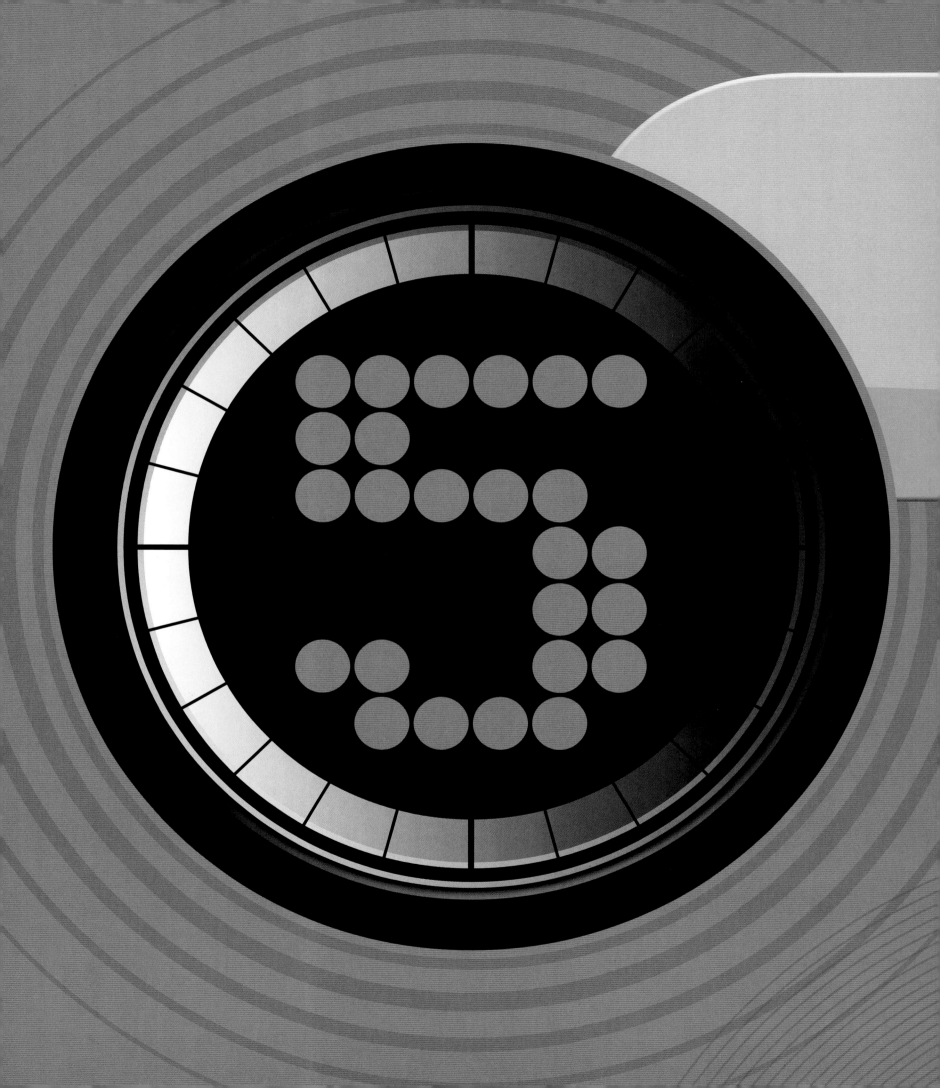

# EXPLORING THE DEEP

The ocean is the last great unexplored part of our planet. We have little idea of what lies beneath the waves, let alone how many species there are or how they live. The only way to find out is to go down there and get up close—even if some of the animals that live there are really scary.

# OCEAN DEPTHS

**The Earth's continents** are rimmed by stretches of rocky shelf but then plunge straight down into the deep sea. As the water gets deeper, it gets darker and the pressure increases. At the surface, it is icy near the poles and warmer near the equator, but deeper down it is always cold. Many ocean animals live at certain depths, but some swim from zone to zone.

## VERTICAL MIGRATION

Tiny floating animals that live as part of the plankton gather at different depths in the water. Many of them avoid bright light, coming to the surface at night then sinking deeper during the day. Predators who feed on these animals, such as the giant filter-feeding basking shark, have to move up and down in the water as they follow their food.

## In the zone

The ocean's sunlit surface is packed with rich and colorful life, but fewer and stranger animals live at greater depths. Deep-sea animals need special features to survive in the cold darkness.

**SUNLIGHT ZONE**
0–655 ft (0–200 m)

**TWILIGHT ZONE**
655–3,300 ft
(200–1,000 m)

**MIDNIGHT ZONE**
3,300–13,100 ft
(1,000–4,000 m)

## THE SUNLIGHT ZONE

Speedy predators with good vision hunt near the brightly lit ocean surface. Some live near coasts on reefs or among eelgrass, but others prefer to wander the open seas.

Caribbean reef sharks cruise over eelgrass

Frilled sharks prey on squid in the gloom of the twilight zone

## THE TWILIGHT ZONE

The light here is too dim for algae to grow, but is just good enough for animals to see. The rarely seen frilled shark prowls these depths, alongside fish who can make their own light.

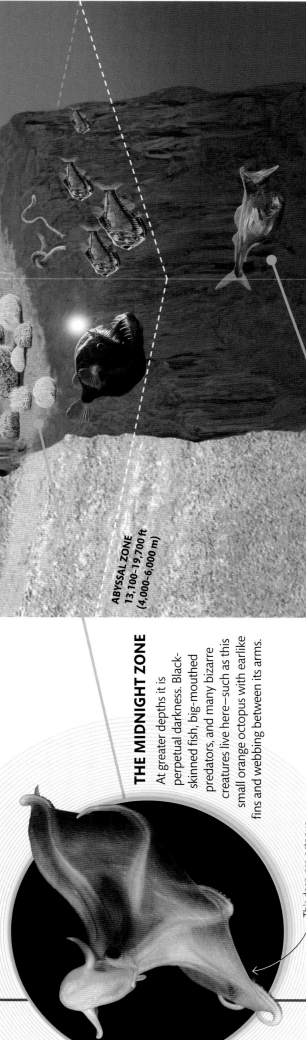
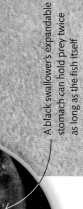
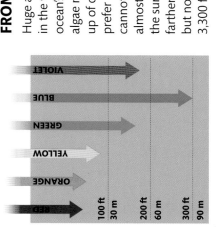

Animals living here have flabby bodies and flexible skeletons to cope with the crushing water pressure

Ocean trenches are the deepest parts of the ocean—very little life exists here, but some trenches have been visited by humans in submersibles

**ABYSSAL ZONE**
**13,100–19,700 ft (4,000–6,000 m)**

A black swallower's expandable stomach can hold prey twice as long as the fish itself

## THE MIDNIGHT ZONE

At greater depths it is perpetual darkness. Black-skinned fish, big-mouthed predators, and many bizarre creatures live here—such as this small orange octopus with earlike fins and webbing between its arms.

This deep-sea octopus uses its webbed arms to envelop prey

## THE ABYSS

Many animals that live in the deepest parts of the ocean eat bits of dead animals sinking down from above, but the black swallower catches live prey. It slowly gulps its victim down whole, coiling it tightly inside its sacklike stomach. It can survive without another meal for a long time.

## FROM LIGHT TO DARK

Huge amounts of tiny green algae in the water provide a feast for the ocean's vegetarians. To make food, algae need sunlight, which is made up of different colors. Most algae prefer the energy of red light, but this cannot reach very far, so algae and almost all other ocean life live near the surface. Blue light can penetrate farther, giving the ocean its color, but no light reaches deeper than 3,300 ft (1,000 m).

VIOLET
BLUE
GREEN
YELLOW
ORANGE
RED

100 ft / 30 m
200 ft / 60 m
300 ft / 90 m

# LIVING IN THE COMMUNITY
## CORAL REEF

**Coral reefs are richer with life** than anywhere else in the ocean. Here, basking in the tropical sunshine, hundreds of different species of corals grow and provide a habitat for thousands of snails, fish, and other animals. Some creatures graze on the coral, whereas others are hungry predators. Other animals even form partnerships and help each other survive.

### UNDERWATER GARDEN

A tropical reef can be as vibrant and colorful as any garden. The sea floor is carpeted with an astonishing variety of corals, seaweeds, and sponges. Teeming with life, coral reefs are called rain forests of the sea.

### WORKING TOGETHER

Some animals work together to make their lives easier. This shrimp plucks scraps of food from a moray eel's mouth, giving the eel a teeth-cleaning and getting itself a meal.

Eels provide easy pickings for hungry shrimp

### HUNTING GROUND

Reef sharks are surrounded by so much prey that they don't have to move far to satisfy their big appetite. Many can squeeze between rocks to grab fish that are hiding there.

## STATS AND FACTS

| SIZE | 232,000 sq miles (600,000 sq km) total area of all coral reefs on the planet |
|---|---|

| | sq miles | 100,000 | | 200,000 |
|---|---|---|---|---|
| | sq km | 200,000 | 400,000 | 600,000 |

138,220 sq miles (358,000 sq km) Great Barrier Reef

The Great Barrier Reef off northern Australia is the biggest reef in the world. It is even visible from space. New species of fish are found there each year.

**GREAT BARRIER REEF**

400 coral species

1,500 fish species

SHARK SPECIES ON REEFS

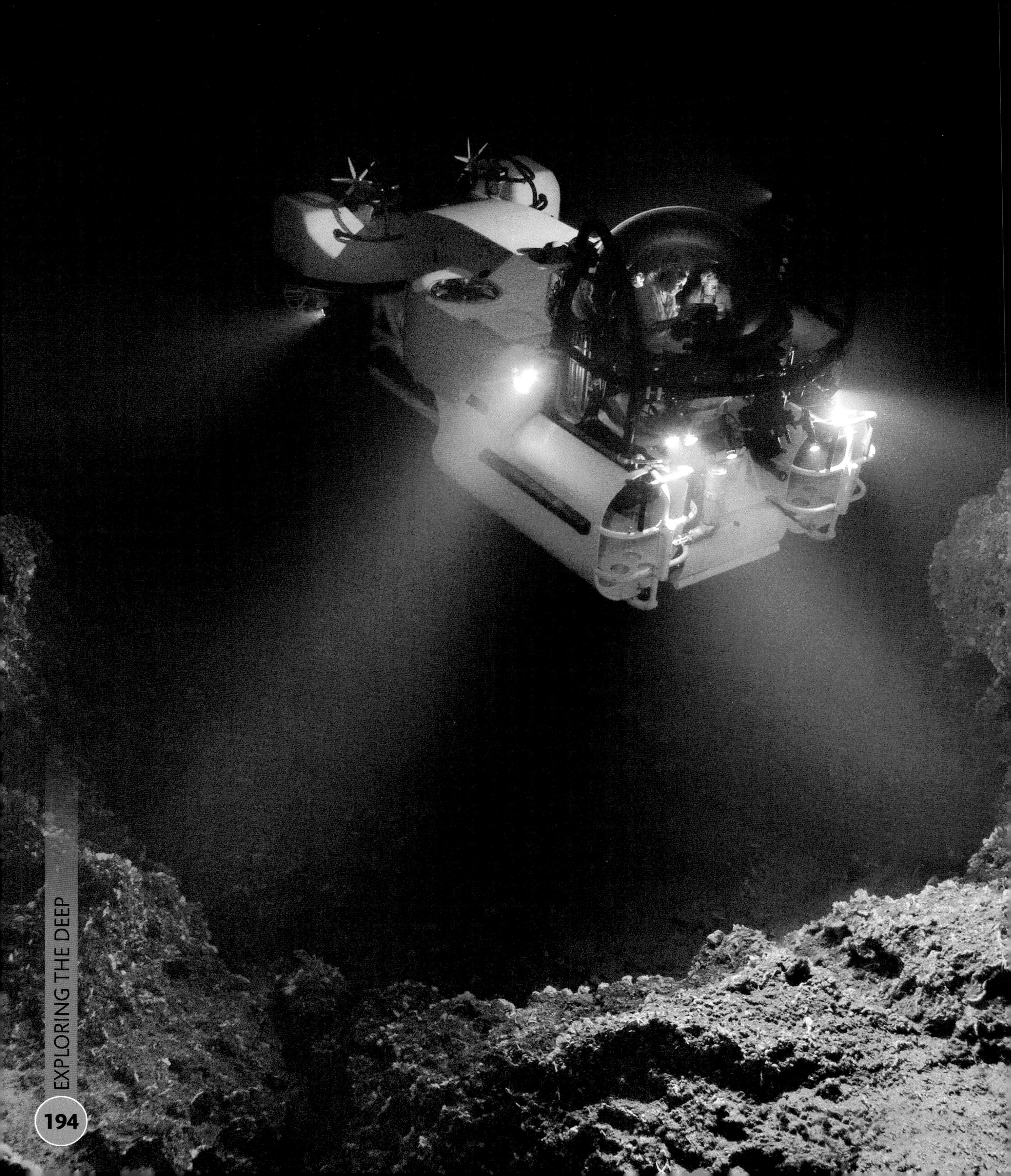

SHINING A LIGHT

Modern submersibles are operated by a three-man crew and are agile enough to explore many parts of the ocean. Big windows and a source of light help make the view as clear as possible.

# DIVE, DIVE, DIVE!

## SUBMERSIBLES

**In 1960 a diving vehicle** called a submersible took a two-man team nearly 7 miles (11 km) down into an underwater trench at the bottom of the Pacific Ocean. To this day, no one has gone as deep, but different submersibles around the world have completed hundreds of deep-sea explorations. Submersibles are reinforced to withstand the high pressures, enabling humans to explore life in the deep ocean.

### DEEP-SEA SMOKERS

Scientists diving in *Alvin*—the best known of all the submersibles in use—were the first to see the strange animals that live around hot, underwater volcanic vents known as black smokers.

*Alvin*'s robot arm takes the temperature of a vent

### OUTSIDE THE SUB

Modern suits made from lightweight aluminum help divers go deeper for longer, but they are not strong enough to go as deep as a crew-carrying submersible.

## STATS AND FACTS

Submersibles have taken humans to the bottom of the ocean. They can dive far deeper than whales, the deepest-diving mammals.

**DEPTH**

14,764 ft (4,500 m) max. depth of *Alvin*

| ft | 10,000 | 20,000 | 30,000 | |
|---|---|---|---|---|
| m | 4,000 | 8,000 | | 12,000 |

35,797 ft (10,911 m) max. depth of US Navy *Trieste*

**DIVE DEPTH**

9,816 ft (2,992 m) deepest dive of any mammal

| ft | 4,000 | 8,000 | |
|---|---|---|---|
| m | 1,000 | 2,000 | 3,000 |

1,089 ft (332 m) deepest scuba dive

DIVES MADE BY ALVIN

**175**
PER YEAR

# GETTING UP CLOSE
## DIVING

**Trained human freedivers can hold their breath** for minutes underwater, but with the right equipment this can stretch to over an hour. Scuba divers use a tank filled with compressed air that is fed to the diver through a mouthpiece. Scuba gear enables many people to dive for fun, and allows scientists to spend enough time in the water to study the ocean and the life that lives there.

### BEHIND BARS

Protection in a cage is the only safe way to get close to great white sharks. The bars are strong enough to withstand the force of sharks crashing into them.

Bull shark accepts a tasty morsel from a metal-gloved diver

### FEEDING TIME

Some predatory sharks are approachable enough for divers to get up close and even feed them with scraps of food. Divers are always careful and treat these animals with respect.

### LIGHTS, CAMERA, ACTION!

Underwater filming isn't easy. Cameras have to be waterproof and you may need extra light to film in deep water. The really tricky part is getting your stars to cooperate so that you can get the perfect shot.

### SWIMMING WITH GIANTS

The world's biggest shark, the whale shark, is a harmless filter feeder and stays so close to the surface that snorkelers can swim alongside this gentle giant.

# HIDDEN IN THE DEPTHS
## SHIPWRECKS

**There are around three million shipwrecks** lying on the ocean bed and the oldest have been there for more than three thousand years. Ships sink as a result of accidents at sea and the cold, salty water helps prevent decay. Marine life soon takes over as corals grow on the wrecks and fish arrive. Over time, many other species make shipwrecks their home until this new habitat is crowded with all sorts of ocean life.

Sharks look for easy meals

### RICH PICKINGS

The wide variety of life found on a wreck attracts big predators that make the most of available prey. Reef sharks patrol older shipwrecks that are home to smaller animals.

### SAFE HAVEN

A shipwreck provides shelter for ocean animals, hiding them from bigger predators. Animals use them the same way they would use natural caves and rocky crevices.

An old bottle makes a safe home

### UNDER INVESTIGATION

Marine biologists are interested in understanding how life can colonize wrecks. Archaeologists use shipwrecks to study how humans lived and used the oceans many years ago.

### TAKING OVER

Anemones, barnacles, and sea urchins are among the first animals to set up home on a sunken ship. About a year or two later, corals start building up, turning the shipwreck into an artificial reef.

199

# DESCENT INTO DARKNESS
## BOTTOM OF THE SEA

**The surface of the ocean** is bright with sunshine, wild with waves and, in the tropics, it is warm. Deeper down, the Sun's rays cannot reach: it is always dark and colder than inside a refrigerator. The deepest part of the ocean is home to some of the strangest animals on the planet. There is so little food down there that fish swim slowly to save their energy. Anything that comes within range is a potential meal—even if it's bigger than you are.

### GLOWING IN THE DARK

Many deep-sea animals have special light-producing organs or patches in their skin. They flash their lights to signal to mates, or use them as a lure for attracting prey.

Giant tube worms, crabs, and fish live around hot water vents on the sea floor

### HOT-BED OF LIFE

In places the ocean floor has volcanic ridges that spew out super-hot water. The animals here survive the high temperatures and feed on chemicals dissolved in the water.

Mouthlike hood snaps shut when food drifts inside

### UNDER PRESSURE

Some animals, such as this predatory tunicate, live attached to the ocean floor. It catches tiny floating animals in its "jaws" and, like other deep-sea animals, has a flabby body that can withstand the high water pressure.

**GHOST OF THE DEEP**
This ghost shark is happiest in coastal seas but sometimes descends to deeper, darker waters where it spends most of its time swimming slowly along the bottom looking for equally slow prey. Its strong sense of smell and ability to detect electric fields help it search in the gloom.

**HELPING A FRIEND**

Manatees are slow-moving mammals that can be injured by collisions with ships and other motorboats. They are also harmed by pollution. Scientists keep a check on their numbers to see if they need extra protection.

# KEEPING TRACK
## PROTECTING THE SEAS

**The ocean looks so vast** that it seems endless and everlasting. In fact, many animals are fished so much that their numbers are dropping. Garbage from land pollutes the water, while ocean life is harmed by climate changes. All around the world people are studying the ocean and doing what they can to protect the animals that live there and prevent them from being driven to extinction.

Radio tracker fixed to turtle's shell

### TRACKING MOVEMENTS

By fitting animals with trackers that send out detectable signals, scientists can keep track of where they go. This helps them protect species that rely on certain habitats to survive.

### REPLANTING REEFS

In places where reefs have been destroyed, special frames are used to replace them. These have been "seeded" with fragments of coral, encouraging the growth of new reefs as habitats for animals.

## STATS AND FACTS

Scientists are still discovering new types of marine life. There could be as many as one million species living in the ocean.

**NUMBER OF SPECIES DESCRIBED PER YEAR**

136 fish    452 crustaceans    683 other
379 mollusks    Total 1,650

**NUMBER OF FISH SPECIES**

17,400 species of marine fish

32,800 total fish species

RECORDED MARINE SPECIES

200,000

# GLOSSARY

**ABYSS**
The abyss, or abyssal zone, is the deepest part of the ocean, stretching 13,100 to 19,700 ft (4,000–6,000 m). It is intensely dark and cold and few animals are able to live there.

**ALGAE**
A group of simple plants that include microscopic green plankton and enormous multicelled seaweeds, such as giant kelp.

**BELL**
The umbrella-shaped body of a jellyfish.

**BIOLUMINESCENCE**
The production of light by animals. It can be used to attract a mate, for camouflage, as a decoy, for catching prey, or for communication. It is created by a chemical reaction in the animal's body.

**BUOYANCY**
The ability of a marine organism to float in water.

**CAMOUFLAGE**
Colors and patterns on an animal's skin that help it blend in with its surroundings.

**CANINE**
A pointed tooth that is often enlarged in meat eaters and is used for tearing food. In walruses and narwhals the upper canines grow long enough to form tusks.

**CARTILAGE**
A tough, light yet flexible substance that makes up the skeleton of a shark or ray instead of bone.

**COLD-BLOODED**
Describes an animal whose body temperature varies with that of its environment. It controls its temperature by moving to hotter or cooler areas as needed.

**COLONY**
A group of animals that live closely together, often relying on each other. Corals live in colonies.

**CORAL**
Soft-bodied animals that live in large groups or colonies, usually in warm, shallow seas. They secrete a substance that hardens into stone around them for protection.

**CRUSTACEAN**
An animal such as a shrimp, crab, or lobster that has a hard outer shell and four or more pairs of limbs. They have to molt the outer shell to grow.

**DECIBEL**
A unit that measures the intensity or loudness of a sound. Total silence is just above 0 decibels (dB).

**DISK WIDTH**
Term used to describe the body size of a fish, such as a ray, that has "wings."

**DORSAL FIN**
An unpaired, upright fin on the back of a fish, whale, or dolphin.

**ECHINODERM**
A marine invertebrate that has a chalky outer skeleton and tube feet, such as a sea star (starfish) or sea urchin.

**ELECTRORECEPTION**
The ability of an aquatic animal to detect an electric field or current. It is used for detecting objects or for communication.

**EGG CASE**
The tough case that surrounds the fertilized egg of some sharks or rays. It protects the developing shark until it is ready to hatch.

**ESTUARY**
The mouth of a large river at the point where it meets the sea. The amount of salt in the water changes with the tide.

**FEEDING FRENZY**
When a group of predators, such as sharks or sailfish, work together to herd and attack prey, often with few of the prey surviving.

**FEELER**
Part of the body that is used to sense or touch things, especially when searching for food.

**FILTER FEEDER**
An animal that feeds by filtering out plankton or small particles of food suspended in water.

**FLATFISH**
A flattened species of fish that swims on its side, close to the seabed. Both eyes lie on the same side of the head. Members of this group include plaice, soles, and halibut.

**GAPE**
The wide opening of an animal's mouth or shell.

**GESTATION**
The period of time, also called a pregnancy, between the fertilization of an egg and the birth of an animal.

**GILLS**
The structures used by fish and other aquatic animals to obtain oxygen from water. Usually arranged in pairs, they also get rid of waste carbon dioxide from the blood.

**HERTZ**
A unit (Hz) used to measure the frequency of sound waves. One hertz is equal to one cycle per second. The higher the frequency of cycles, the higher-pitched the sound.

**HYDROTHERMAL VENT**
A crack in the seabed that pours out superheated water that is full of minerals. Vents are often home to unique colonies of animals that can survive in harsh conditions.

**INVERTEBRATE**
An animal without a backbone. Includes corals, mollusks, starfish, jellyfish, shrimp, and sponges.

**JUVENILE**
A young animal that is not yet able to reproduce.

**LARVA**
A young stage of an animal that looks very different from its adult form. Many marine animals spend part of their early life as a larva, including crabs, corals, and lobsters. (Plural is *larvae*.)

**LURE**
A part of the body of a marine animal that is used as bait to attract another animal when hunting. Lures can resemble a food animal, such as a worm, or be bioluminescent to attract prey in darkness.

**MAMMAL**
A warm-blooded animal that has hair and feeds its young on milk. Marine mammals include whales, dolphins, and seals.

**MEMBRANE**
A thin, flexible piece of skinlike tissue that acts as a barrier.

**MIDNIGHT ZONE**
The cold, dark zone in the middle of the ocean. It generally describes depths between 3,300–13,100 ft (1,000 and 4,000 m) below the surface. Animals that live here have to cope with intense pressure and constant darkness.

**MIGRATION**
The regular return journey that an animal makes every year to reach feeding or breeding grounds.

**MOLLUSK**
An invertebrate animal that has a soft, muscular body. Sometimes the body is surrounded by a hard shell. Mollusks include snails, clams, and sea slugs.

**MOLT**
The process of shedding an outer layer of skin or an external shell so that an animal can grow. This occurs at certain times of the year or at particular points in the animal's life cycle.

**MOUTHBROODER**
Species of fish in which one of the parents holds the developing eggs in its mouth until they hatch. During this time the adult cannot feed.

**NOCTURNAL**
Describes an animal that is active at night and sleeps during the day.

**NUTRIENT**
A substance that provides vital nourishment needed for the growth and maintenance of life.

**OCEAN TRENCH**
A very deep canyon in the ocean floor. The temperature is barely above freezing and the water pressure is crushing. Few animals can survive here.

**PARASITE**
An organism that lives on or inside another animal to gain food or shelter. It is usually harmful to its host.

**PECTORAL FINS**
A pair of fins that lie either side of a fish's head that help control its direction of movement.

**PITCH**
The high or low quality of a sound.

**PLANKTON**
Tiny animals and algae that drift or float in the sea and other water bodies. They provide food for larger animals.

**PREDATOR**
An animal that hunts and kills other animals (its prey) for food.

**PREY**
An animal that is killed and eaten by a predator.

**PROPULSION**
The action of moving forward.

**RAKER**
A structure in a filter-feeding fish that scrapes food particles off the gills and diverts them to the food pipe.

**REEF**
A ridge of jagged coral, rock, or sand lying just above or below the surface of the sea.

**REPTILE**
A cold-blooded vertebrate with scaly, waterproof skin, such as a marine iguana or a sea snake.

**SALINITY**
The amount of salt dissolved in water. Seawater has 35 g of salt for every liter of water. Fresh water is usually less than 0.5 g of salt per liter.

**SCAVENGER**
An animal that feeds on dead plants or animals.

**SCHOOL OR SHOAL**
A large number of fish that swim together.

**SENSORY PORE**
Part of a network of jelly-filled pockets on the skin of sharks and other electroreceptive fish. These pores help fish detect electric fields.

**SKELETON**
A framework of bone or cartilage that supports the body of an animal and provides attachment points for muscles.

**SKIN PIGMENT**
Color found in the skin of an animal.

**SLIME**
A soft and slippery substance that is produced by the skin of an animal. It helps fish swim more easily, but also protects them against parasites and infections. Some slimes are poisonous to predators.

**SPAWN**
The eggs of a fish, amphibian, or invertebrate. Spawning is the laying of the eggs.

**SPECIES**
A group of animals that look like one another and can reproduce with each other—animals cannot reproduce with members of another species.

**STINGER**
A weapon used by some animals in self-defense or to capture prey by injecting a poison through a hollow spine or harpoon.

**SUBMERSIBLE**
A small underwater craft designed for research and exploration.

**SUNLIGHT ZONE**
The uppermost layer of the ocean, which is bathed with sunlight during the day. In clear water it can extend down as far as 655 ft (200 m); in murky water as little as 50 ft (15 m). Most fish live in this zone.

**TENTACLE**
Thin, flexible limb mainly used for grasping and feeding. Some carry sense organs for touch, taste, smell, or vision. Others may be equipped with suckers, stingers, hooks, or even teeth.

**TIDE**
The twice-daily rise and fall in sea level that is caused by the pull of the Sun and Moon.

**TOXIC**
Describes a substance that is poisonous. The bite or sting of an animal may have a toxic effect on another animal.

**TWILIGHT ZONE**
The region immediately below the sunlight zone, from 655 to 3,300 ft (200–1,000 m). Very little light reaches this level and plants cannot grow.

**WARM-BLOODED**
Describes an animal that is able to keep its body temperature constant regardless of the temperature of its surroundings. All marine mammals and some sharks are warm-blooded.

**WATER PRESSURE**
The weight of the water pressing down on an animal as it goes deeper into the ocean. At the bottom of the deepest trench it is as much as 8 tons per square inch (1 tonne per square cm).

**VENOM**
A poison, or toxin, produced by an animal that is used in hunting or self-defense. It is injected into another animal through a bite or sting.

**VERTEBRATE**
An animal that has a backbone or spinal column made up of individual bones or pieces of cartilage called vertebrae. (Single is *vertebra*.)

**VERTICAL MIGRATION**
A pattern of movement of animals (and plankton) between deep and shallow waters. This may happen daily or be seasonal. It also occurs in animals that spend different stages of their lives at different depths.

---

**ABBREVIATIONS USED IN THIS BOOK**

| | |
|---|---|
| / | per—for example, km/h means kilometers per hour |
| °C | degrees Celsius |
| cal | calories |
| cm | centimeter |
| dB | decibel |
| °F | degrees Fahrenheit |
| fl oz | fluid ounce |
| ft | foot |
| g | gram |
| Hz | hertz—see glossary for definition |
| in | inch |
| kg | kilogram |
| km | kilometer |
| lb | pound |
| m | meter |
| min | minute |
| ml | milliliter |
| mm | millimeter |
| mph | miles per hour |
| oz | ounce |
| s or sec | second |
| sq | square |

# INDEX

# ACKNOWLEDGMENTS

**Dorling Kindersley** would like to thank Alex Lloyd, Simon Murrell, Amy Child, Clare Joyce, Richard Biesty, Vanya Mittal, Sanjay Chauhan, and Sudakshina Basu for design assistance; Frankie Piscitelli, Vineetha Mokkil, Suefa Lee, Deeksha Saikia, and Rohan Sinha for editorial assistance; Liz Moore for additional picture research; Katie John for proofreading; Hilary Bird for the index; Steve Crozier for creative retouching; and Peter Bull for additional illustration.

DK would also like to thank Simon Christopher, Jason Isley, and Gil Woolley at Scubazoo for providing photographs and consultancy advice. Scubazoo specialize in filming and photographing life under the sea, and take an active role in marine conservation projects all over the world. **www.scubazoo.com**

The publisher would like to thank the following for their kind permission to reproduce their photographs:

(Key: a-above; b-below/bottom; c-center; f-far; l-left; r-right; t-top)

**1 OceanwideImages.com:** C & M Fallows. **4 Photoshot:** Charles Hood (tc). **Scubazoo. com:** Adam Broadbent (tr). **5 Scubazoo. com:** Jason Isley (tl, tr, tc). **10-11 Photoshot:** Charles Hood. **10 Photoshot:** Charles Hood (cl). **12-13 Scubazoo.com:** Jason Isley. **13 Scubazoo.com:** Roger Munns (cr). **14 Alamy Images:** WaterFrame (cl). **15 Corbis:** Stuart Westmorland (br). **16 Getty Images:** Jeff Rotman / Photolibrary (bl). **17 Dreamstime.com:** Greg Amptman (tl). **Getty Images:** Mark Conlin / Oxford Scientific (bl). **19 FLPA:** Minden Pictures / Norbert Wu (tl). **20-21 Getty Images:** Paul Nicklen. **23 Corbis:** Minden Pictures / Norbert Wu (bl). **24-25 Dreamstime.com:** Kkg1. **25 Photoshot:** Picture Alliance (cr). **26 Auscape:** John Lewis (cl). **27 Corbis:** Kevin Fleming (tr); Lynda Richardson (bc). **28-29 Scubazoo.com:** Roger Munns. **30-31 OceanwideImages.com:** Andy Murch. **30 SuperStock:** Mark Conlin (cl). **33 Getty Images:** Nature, underwater and art photos. www.Narchuk.com / Moment Open (crb). **34 Getty Images:** Doug Allan / Oxford Scientific (cra). **SuperStock:** Minden Pictures (c). **36 Scubazoo.com:** Jason Isley (cl, tr). **38-39 Getty Images:** David Jenkins / Robert Harding World Imagery.

**40-41 Scubazoo.com:** Adam Broadbent. **40 Scubazoo.com:** Jason Isley (cl). **43 FLPA:** Biosphoto / Jean-Michel Mille (br). **Scubazoo.com:** Jason Isley (tr). **44-45 Corbis:** Steve Jones / Stocktrek Images. **44 Scubazoo.com:** Jason Isley (cl). **46-47 Alamy Images:** Norbert Probst / Imagebroker. **47 123RF.com:** Krzysztof Odziomek (cr). **48 Corbis:** Alex Kerstitch / Visuals Unlimited (b). **49 Alamy Images:** Blickwinkel (c). **Photoshot:** NHPA (cra). **51 Dorling Kindersley:** David Peart (cl). **52-53 Alamy Images:** Steve Bloom Images. **52 Alamy Images:** Steve Bloom Images (cl). **54 Corbis:** Water Rights / Christophe Courteau (cl). **55 Corbis:** Brandon D. Cole (bl). **Photoshot:** Nigel Downer (cra). **56-57 Science Photo Library:** Alexander Semenov. **56 Dreamstime.com:** Steven Melanson (cl). **59 FLPA:** Biosphoto / Mike Veitch (tc). **Scubazoo.com:** Adam Broadbent (cb). **60-61 imagequestmarine.com:** Michael Aw. **62-63 Science Photo Library:** Dante Fenolio. **63 Science Photo Library:** Dante Fenolio (cr). **66-67 FLPA:** Martin Hale. **66 Corbis:** Hiroya Minakuchi / Minden Pictures (cl). **68-69 Getty Images:** Alexander Safonov / Moment Select. **68 Scubazoo.com:** Roger Munns (cl). **70 FLPA:** Minden Pictures / Pete Oxford (tc). **72-73 Corbis:** Andy Murch / Visuals Unlimited. **73 Scubazoo.com:** Jason Isley (cr). **74-75 Alamy Images:** WaterFrame. **76-77 Scubazoo.com:** Adam Broadbent. **77 Scubazoo.com:** Jason Isley (cr). **78-79 FLPA:** Norbert Probst / Imagebroker. **79 Scubazoo.com:** Jason Isley (cr). **80-81 Alamy Images:** Anthony Pierce. **82-83 Getty Images:** Masa Ushioda. **84-85 Science Photo Library:** Christopher Swann. **85 Scubazoo.com:** Jason Isley (cr). **86-87 SeaPics.com:** Doug Perrine. **87 Corbis:** Stuart Westmorland (cr). **88-89 Photoshot:** Andy Rouse. **89 Getty Images:** Danita Delimont / Gallo Images (cr). **92-93 Scubazoo.com:** Gil Woolley. **93 Scubazoo.com:** Jason Isley (cr). **94-95 SeaPics.com:** Doug Perrine. **94 Scubazoo.com:** Jason Isley (cl). **96-97 Scubazoo.com:** Jason Isley. **97 FLPA:** Ingo Arndt / Minden Pictures (cr). **98 Alamy Images:** National Geographic Image Collection (cra). **99 Alamy Images:** Karen & Ian Stewart (tr). **Robert Harding Picture Library:** Michael S. Nolan (crb). **100 Scubazoo.com:** Jason Isley (cl).

**100-101 Scubazoo.com:** Adam Broadbent. **102-103 Scubazoo.com:** Jason Isley. **104-105 imagequestmarine.com:** James D. Watt. **106-107 Corbis:** Chris Newbert / Minden Pictures. **107 Scubazoo. com:** Adam Broadbent (cr). **108-109 FLPA:** Bruno Guenard / Biosphoto. **110-111 Corbis:** Paul Nicklen / National Geographic Society. **112-113 naturepl.com:** Bruce Rasner / Rotman. **115 Getty Images:** Borut Furlan / WaterFrame (br). **117 Getty Images:** Doug Perrine / Photolibrary. **118 Scubazoo.com:** Gil Woolley (br). **119 Science Photo Library:** Paul Zahl (cl). **120-121 Scubazoo.com:** Jason Isley. **121 Getty Images:** Gerard Soury / Oxford Scientific (cr). **122 Dreamstime.com:** Howard Chew / Singularone (cl). **122-123 Scubazoo.com:** Jason Isley. **124-125 Photoshot. 125 FLPA:** Kelvin Aitken (cr). **127 Corbis:** Chris Newbert / Minden Pictures (tl). **128-129 Science Photo Library:** Visuals Unlimited Inc. / Andy Murch. **129 FLPA:** Biosphoto / Gérard Soury (cr). **130-131 Alamy Images:** FLPA. **131 Scubazoo.com:** Jason Isley (cr). **132-133 Scubazoo.com:** Jason Isley. **134-135 FLPA:** Gerry Ellis / Minden Pictures. **134 Getty Images:** David Courtenay / Oxford Scientific (cl). **136-137 Alamy Images:** Mark Conlin. **138 FLPA:** Biosphoto / Brandon Cole (clb); Minden Pictures / Mitsuaki Iwago (cl). **Scubazoo.com:** Christian Loader (tr). **139 Alamy Images:** Martin Strmiska (cr). **140-141 Alamy Images:** WaterFrame. **142-143 Scubazoo.com:** Jason Isley. **144-145 Alamy Images:** Dan Sullivan. **145 Photoshot:** Charles Hood / Oceans Image (cr). **146-147 Robert Harding Picture Library:** Reinhard Dirscherl. **147 Alamy Images:** Photoshot Holdings Ltd (cr). **148 Scubazoo.com:** Jason Isley (cl). **148-149 Scubazoo.com:** Christian Loader (cr). **150-151 Getty Images:** David Wrobel / Visuals Unlimited, Inc. **151 Photoshot:** NHPA (cr). **152-153 Getty Images:** Marevision. **154-155 Photoshot:** Saul Gonor / Oceans Image. **156-157 Getty Images:** Visuals Unlimited, Inc. / Reinhard Dirscherl. **156 Alamy Images:** Adam Butler (cl). **158-159 Getty Images:** Barcroft Media / Contributor. **160-161 Getty Images:** Sakis Papadopoulos / The Image Bank. **164 Alamy Images:** Martin Strmiska (br). **Photoshot:** Michael Patrick O'Neill (cl). **165 FLPA:** Imagebroker / Norbert Probst (tr).

**166-167 Naturfoto www.naturephoto-cz.com. 168 Alamy Images:** Marty Snyderman / Stephen Frink Collection (cl). **169 Corbis. 170-171 FLPA:** Hiroya Minakuchi / Minden Pictures. **172 Scubazoo.com:** Jason Isley (tr). **173 Scubazoo.com:** Jason Isley (tr, br). **174-175 SeaPics.com:** Eric Cheng. **176-177 Dreamstime.com:** Beverly Speed. **177 Photoshot:** LOOK (cr). **178-179 Alamy Images:** Tobias Friedrich / F1online digitale Bildagentur GmbH. **178 Scubazoo. com:** Jason Isley (cl). **180 Science Photo Library:** Visuals Unlimited Inc. / Andy Murch (bc). **181 FLPA:** Biosphoto / Bruno Guenard (tr). **182-183 Photoshot:** Richard Smith / NHPA. **184-185 Scubazoo.com:** Jason Isley. **186-187 FLPA:** Imagebroker. **186 Science Photo Library:** Andy Murch / Visuals Unlimited, Inc. (cl). **190 FLPA:** Biosphoto / Pascal Kobeh (cla). **Getty Images:** (crb). **Scubazoo.com:** Jason Isley (bc). **191 imagequestmarine.com:** Peter Herring (cb). **naturepl.com:** David Shale (bl). **192 FLPA:** Biosphoto / Yann Hubert (c). **Scubazoo.com:** Jason Isley (clb). **192-193 Scubazoo.com:** Jason Isley. **194-195 Getty Images:** Brian J. Skerry. **195 Science Photo Library:** Alexis Rosenfeld (cb). **Woods Hole Oceanographic Instititution:** Image courtesy Charles Fisher, Penn State / NSF, NOAA / HOV Alvin 2002 (cr). **196-197 Scubazoo.com:** Jason Isley. **197 Getty Images:** Wayne Lynch (c). **Scubazoo.com:** Adam Broadbent (bc); Jason Isley (crb). **198-199 Science Photo Library:** Photostock-Israel. **198 Corbis:** Stephen Frink (bc, c). **Scubazoo.com:** Jason Isley (clb). **200-201 FLPA:** Minden Pictures / Norbert Wu. **200 FLPA:** Frans Lanting (c); Minden Pictures / Norbert Wu (bc). **Science Photo Library:** Dr. Ken MacDonald (clb). **202-203 Science Photo Library:** Douglas Faulkner. **203 Alamy Images:** Rheinhard Dirscherl (cr). **Scubazoo.com:** Roger Munns (cb). **204 Scubazoo.com:** Jason Isley (tr, ftr); Christian Loader (tc). **206 Scubazoo.com:** Jason Isley (tr, ftr); Roger Munns (tc). **208 Scubazoo.com:** Jason Isley (tr)

Endpapers: **Dreamstime.com:** Dream69 0

All other images © Dorling Kindersley

For further information see: **www.dkimages.com**